The Young Conservative's Field Guide

Facts, Charts and Figures

Brenton Stransky & Andrew Foy, MD

Nimble Books LLC
1521 Martha Avenue
Ann Arbor, MI, USA 48103

http://www.NimbleBooks.com
wfz@nimblebooks.com

+1.734-330-2593

ISBN-13: 9781608880140

Printed in the United States of America

The paper used in this publication meets the minimum requirements of the American National Standard for Information Sciences—Permanence of Paper for Printed Library Materials, ANSI Z39.48-1992. The paper is acid-free and lignin-free.

Contents

ONE
Conservatism   6

TWO
Government Spending   17

THREE
Taxation   53

FOUR
Government Run Healthcare   72

FIVE
Healthcare Solutions   93

SIX
Financial Crises   115

SEVEN
Government Bailouts   146

EIGHT
Climate Change   157

NINE
Responsible Energy Policy   175

TEN
Conclusion   190

AFTERWARD
Notes on Debating   199

About the Authors

Brent Stransky

Brent was hired as the youngest Senior Financial Consultant at a large national investment firm. He manages an exclusive practice and a significant portfolio of investments. He graduated from Susquehanna University with honors, a degree in International Business and was conference all scholastic in football. Brent also studied economics at The London School of Business at Birkbeck College.

Areas of specialty include: investment analysis and economic analysis.

Andrew Foy

Drew is a medical resident at Thomas Jefferson University Hospital in Philadelphia, Pennsylvania and a Captain in the US Army Reserves. He attended medical school at Jefferson Medical College where he received the Jeff Hope Student Award for devotion to the underserved population of Philadelphia. He attended Ursinus College for his undergraduate training and graduated with honors in the fields of biochemistry and molecular biology.

Areas of interest include: political philosophy, medical sciences, health care delivery, climate science and domestic energy policy

The natural progress of things is for liberty to yield and government to gain ground.

- Thomas Jefferson, May 1788

(1)   "The Quotable Founding Fathers", Fall River Press 2008

Chapter
1
Conservatism

con·ser·va·tive

Noun
1. One favoring traditional views and values.
2. A supporter of political conservatism.

Adjective
1. Favoring the preservation of established customs and values.
2. Conventional in style.

val·ue

Noun
1. A principle, standard, or quality considered worthwhile or desirable.

con·ser·va·tism

Noun
1. (Political) philosophy calling for lower taxes, limited government regulation of business and investing, a strong national defense, and individual financial responsibility for personal needs. (1)

What were the values this country was founded upon?

(1) "Conservatism," Merriam-Webster Dictionary, www.merriam-webster.com accessed 10/1/09

Founding Values

Our country was founded on the belief that man has the **right** to his *own life, liberty and pursuit of happiness* which means the freedom of each individual to take all the actions required to support the furtherance, fulfillment and enjoyment of his own life.

The concept of a right pertains only to *freedom of action*. Therefore, for every individual, a right is the moral sanction of his freedom to act on his own judgment, for his own goals, by his own voluntary, uncoerced choice. His rights *impose no obligations on his neighbors*. His neighbors are *only* required to abstain from violating his rights.

Europe seemed incapable of becoming the home of free States. It was from America that the plain ideas that men ought to mind their own business, and that the nation is responsible to Heaven for the acts of State – ideas long locked in the breasts of solitary thinkers, and hidden among Latin folios - burst forth like a conqueror upon the world they were destined to transform, under the title of the Rights of Man.

- Lord Acton

To safeguard these rights, the Founders established a *Republic*, under a written Constitution.

An important distinction must be made between a
Democracy and Republic

These two *forms* of government are not only dissimilar but *antithetical*.

Democracy	Republic
- The majority unlimited - The individual, and any group of individuals composing any minority, have no protection against the unlimited power of the majority - This is true whether it is a direct democracy, or a representative democracy - It is a case of majority-over-man	- The majority limited - A constitutionally limited government of the representative type, created by a written Constitution - People form their governments and grant them *only* limited powers, in order to secure their inalienable rights - It is a case of man-over-majority

The American philosophy and system of government thus bar equally the "snob rule" of a governing elite and the "mob rule" of an omnipotent majority.

A Republic is designed to preclude the existence of any governmental power capable of being misused to violate *the individual's* rights.

The founding fathers proposed a republican type of government; ever mindful not to infringe on the personal liberties of its citizens.

It is a melancholy reflection that liberty should be equally exposed to danger whether the Government have too much or too little power.
- James Madison, October 1788

A wise and frugal government, which shall restrain men from injuring one another, shall leave them otherwise free to regulate their own pursuits of industry and improvement, and shall not take from the mouth of labor the bread it has earned. This is the sum of good government...
- Thomas Jefferson, 1801

Security to the persons and properties of the governed is obviously the design and end of the civil government...
- John Hancock, March 1774

A Constitution of Government once changed from freedom, can never be restored. Liberty once lost is forever lost.
- John Adams, 1775

If we can prevent the government from wasting the labors of the people, under the pretense of taking care of them, they must become happy.
- Thomas Jefferson, March 1802

(1) "The Quotable Founding Fathers", Fall River Press 2008

America at the time of the revolution was a bastion of intellectual thought, attracting the world's foremost thinkers and philosophers. In spite of the country's youth, more people could read and write than in any other country. Four times more newspapers were printed here than in France (which had six times more people). The brightest of these men came to be known as the founding fathers. (1)

At times the framers of our country have come under scrutiny for creating too limited a government that could not possibly adapt to or predict the dimensions our society has taken. These critics believe that our Constitution and Bill of Rights are "living, breathing documents," open to a changing interpretation of their original meaning.

While at first glance a "changing interpretation" may seem reasonable we must remember that the founding fathers were ardent students of 2,000 years of history and past governments. Our constitution provides the means for its own change through "due process" designed to protect its citizens from easy and arbitrary "interpretation" by the current party in power.

It should be noted that most points of "interpretation" have led to a greater influence of government in our lives.

(1) "The Quotable Founding Fathers", Fall River Press 2008

Permanently linked with Liberty is Free Market Capitalism.

Free market capitalism is the <u>only</u> social system based on the recognition of individual rights, in which all property is privately owned and all relationships are voluntary. The economic value of a man's work is determined by one principle: the *voluntary consent* of those who are willing to trade him their work or products in return.

Underlying most arguments against the free market is a lack of belief in freedom itself.

History suggests that capitalism is a necessary condition for political freedom.

- Milton Friedman

If one wishes to advocate a free society - that is, capitalism - one must realize that its indispensable foundation is the principle of individual rights. If one wishes to uphold individual rights, one must realize that capitalism is the only system that can uphold and protect them.

- Ayn Rand

Capitalism also <u>effects the best allocation of resources</u> and as such, represents the best economic system to improve the lives of all members of society.

"Every individual... by pursuing his own interest, frequently promotes that of the society more effectually than when he really intends to promote it. I have never known much good done by those who affected to trade for the public good."

- Adam Smith (1)

This idea is known as
"The Invisible Hand Theory"

Adam Smith

Adam Smith, a Scottish Philosopher and Economist born in 1723, is the father of the "political economy" (the study of interaction of the government and economy).

ADAM SMITH

(1) "The Quotable Founding Fathers", Fall River Press 2008, page 81
(2) Encyclopaedia Britannica, http://www.britannica.com/EBchecked/topic/5496 30/Adam-Smith, accessed 3/9/09
(3) Photo by George Landow, www.thevictoriaweb.com, accessed 2/14/09

From a conservative viewpoint, the role of government is to protect individuals' natural rights through

1. The provision of national defense to protect individuals from foreign invaders.
2. The provision of Civil defense to protect individuals from injuring one another.
3. The provision of a court system to enforce the rule of law in adherence with an objective set of standards and to enforce voluntary contracts entered in a free capitalist market.

Our Founders clearly established a government whose role was limited …

> We the people of the United States, in order to form a more perfect union, establish justice, insure domestic tranquility, provide for the common defense, promote the general welfare, and secure the blessings of liberty to ourselves and our posterity, do ordain and establish this Constitution for the United States of America.
> - "The Constitution of the USA," Federal Convention, 1787

Through this book we will endeavor to show why conservatism will protect individual liberty and provide a better quality of life than liberalism.

You might like to know...

The definition and history of conservatism as a political philosophy vary widely between countries. Most historians attribute the first observation of conservatism to the Irishman Edmund Burke who, in his influential work "Reflections on the Revolution in France" (1790), rejected the radical nature of "revolution" and instead proposed that governmental change should be "evolutionary," with "a disposition to preserve and an ability to improve..." *(1)*

To best understand the evolution of conservatism in the US we might start with a brief history of the major political parties and political philosophies of the US.

Federalists: The First Political Party

Early political debate in the US was dominated by fighting between those who proposed a strong central government (Federalists) and those who believed that states should retain more power (Anti-Federalists). The Federalists, led by George. Washington, John Adams and Alexander Hamilton dominated early debate but by 1820 the Federalist Party had lost relevancy.

(1) "Conservatism," Encyclopaedia Britannica, http://www.britannica.com/EBchecked/ topic/133435/ conservatism, Accessed 9/21/09
(2) "Federalist Essays," http://www.loc.gov/rr/program/bib/ourdocs/Images/ federalist.jpg, Accessed 9/21/09

Both the modern Democrat and Republican parties can trace their origins to Thomas Jefferson, who founded the Democratic Republican party (today's Democrats) in 1792 to oppose the Federalists.

Ironically, the Jeffersonian Democratic-Republicans (today's Democrats) were founded on the principles of a decentralized government with limited power and a bill of rights to protect individual rights from an overly powerful government; far different from the party's current platform of bigger government and more social programs. After the demise of the Federalist Party soon after the turn of the century, the Democratic-Republicans became so dominant that their 1820 candidate for president, James Monroe, ran un-opposed.

As a testament to the original philosophy of the Democratic party, Monroe strongly believed that Federal spending on domestic projects (except infrastructure) was unconstitutional! (1) The 1824 election between four Democratic-Republicans (most notably Andrew Jackson and John Quincy Adams) caused the schism into the more recognizable parties of today. Adams won the election though Jackson had more popular and electoral votes.

The unrest that followed the 1824 election resulted in a party split; Adams would lead the "National Republicans" and Jackson would lead the "Democrats."

While the Democratic party would progress unchanged in name, the National Republicans became the "Whig" party in 1836 only to eventually disband and join the fledgling "Republican" party that officially started in 1854 progressing until today unchanged in name.

(1) "The Founding Fathers," John S. Bowman, JG Press, 2005
(2) "Conservatism," Encyclopaedia Britannica,
    http://www.britannica.com/EBchecked/topic/133435/ conservatism, Accessed 9/21/09

Chapter 2

Bureaucracy, Entitlement Programs and

Government Spending

"The most important change which extensive government control produces is a psychological change, an alteration in the character of the people. This is necessarily a slow affair, a process which extends not over a few years but perhaps over one or two generations." – F.A. Hayek

Friedrich Hayek (1899-1992) was an important Austrian-born English political economist and 1974 Nobel laureate in economics. He spent much of his lifetime exposing the inequities of socialism and the welfare state.

1. The current level of government spending is significantly higher than the "Optimum Level" impeding economic growth and prosperity. (pages 20 – 27)

2. Government spending, especially for entitlement programs, is increasing at an unsustainable rate and will be our generation's burden. (pages 28-34)

3. It is by no means constitutional to redistribute wealth through social programs and our founding fathers painstakingly worded the constitution as such. (pages 37 and 38)

4. Social Security is the biggest example of a failed entitlement program in our county. (pages 42-50)

The size and scope of our government has increased exponentially over the past 100 years, growing to a point where it constricts personal liberties and the workings of our free market economy.

Between the extremes of no government and a totalitarian state, there is a point of balance where optimization is obtained.

The
OPTIMUM Government

A government too large restricts individual freedom and reduces prosperity!

Optimal Government Theory holds that up to a certain point, or "Optimum Level," government expenditures protect individual freedom and increase economic output (GDP) and hence the general welfare.

Freedom is maintained and economic output is enhanced by the provision for :
- The national and local defense;
- A judicial system to protect private property and enforce contracts;
- Infrastructure to facilitate commerce

Point of Optimization

Beyond this *optimal size,* the government begins to drain productive capacity from the private sector. It extorts individual's property, decreases individuals' incentives to be productive and decreases private investment which is responsible for business growth. From this point, increases in the size of government begin to constrict individual liberty and have a negative impact on GDP growth.

Beyond an optimum level, increased government spending and increased taxation reduce economic production!

(1) Caragata, P.J. From Welfare State to the Optimal Size of Government: A Paradigm Shift for Public Policy. *Agenda* 1998;5(3):277-87.

The
OPTIMUM Government

This book will revolve around a central idea; The paradigm of
the Optimum Government

A government <u>too small</u> to establish the rule of law and protect people and their property from both foreign and domestic enemies is less than optimal.

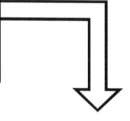

"The Optimum Government"
is the point just before a government becomes so large that it reduces individual freedom, the rate of economic growth and job creation. You could also say that it's the size of government that "optimizes" individual freedom and the free <u>market!</u>

A government <u>too large</u> (socialistic) leads to tyranny and economic stagnation.

(1) Rahn R. The Optimum Government. www.cato.org/ pub_display.p hp?pub_id=9918

For fiscal year 2008, the United States gross domestic product (GDP) was **$14.311trillion** and total Government spending equaled **$5.237 trillion.** (1)

In 2008, total government spending was equivalent to 36% of GDP!

But

In 2009,
Total GDP is estimated
$14.240 T
Total Government
Spending (Fed + State)
will be $6.143.7 T.(2)

OR

43%
of GDP

(1) "A New Era of Responsibility, Renewing America's Promise", Office of Management and Budget, 2010 Budget, http:// www.gpoaccess.gov/usbudget/fy10/pdf/fy10-newera.pdf, accessed 3/14/09
(2) "Highlights of U.S. Federal Budget" various years, Christopher Chantrill, http://www.usgovernmentspending.com/budget_gs.php, accessed 3/12/09

The
OPTIMUM Government

The size of a country's Government can be measured by comparing it to that country's G.D.P.

In a recently completed paper, economists at the Institute for Market Economics (in Sofia, Bulgaria) have provided new estimates of the optimum size of government, using standard models, with data from 28 countries over the period 1970-2007.

Their conclusion, with 99% probability:

the optimal size of government is
LESS THAN 25% of GDP. (1)

Definition

Gross Domestic Product (or GDP) is the monetary value of all goods and services produced by a country over a certain period. (2)

Per Capita GDP is often used as an *indicator of the standard of living* in an economy, the rationale is that all citizens would benefit from their country's increased economic production.(3)

(1) Rahn R. The Optimum Government. www.cato.org/pub_display.php?pub_id=9918
(2) Investopedia.com, a Forbes Digital Company -
    http://www.investopedia.com/terms/g/gdp.asp, accessed 3/10/09
(3) http://en.wikipedia.org/wiki/Gross_domestic_product. Accessed 2/26/09

The aforementioned study from The Institute for Market Economics is the latest in an impressive line of studies to conclude that government spending in excess of 20-25% of GDP decreases economic growth, job creation and the social welfare of its citizens.

One of the most authoritative studies on the optimum size of government was prepared for the Congressional Joint Economic Committee by Vedder and Gallaway.

GOVERNMENT SIZE AND ECONOMIC GROWTH

by
Richard K. Vedder and
Lowell E. Gallaway
Distinguished Professors of Economics,
Ohio University

Prepared for the
Joint Economic Committee

"The results suggest that for each 1 percent increase in the government share of GDP, the GDP itself falls by about $30 billion ... this suggests that $80 billion in federal spending has associated with it, an output-reducing impact of about $34 billion."

Vedder and Gallaway's study examined the relationship between the **five year economic growth rate** and **government spending** in the United States. The authors found, with **99% certainty**, that over the time period of 1796 to 1996 the **size of the federal government** that optimized economic growth was **11.06%**. Over the time period of 1957 to 1993, with **99% certainty**, the **size of state and local government** that optimized economic growth was **11.42%**.

Therefore, five year economic growth is optimized when **total government spending** is equivalent to **22.48%** of GDP.

Vedder RK, Gallaway LE. Government Size and Economic Growth. The Joint Economic Committee. http://www.house.gov/jec/growth/govtsize/govtsize.pdf. Accessed 8/10/09

In a second study prepared for the Joint Economic Committee

Swartney, Lawson and Holcombe performed an empirical analysis of data from 23 OECD countries and found a **strong negative relationship** between both (a) **the size of government and GDP growth** and (b) increases in government expenditures and GDP growth.

"If government expenditures as a share of GDP in the United States had remained at their 1960 level, real GDP in 1996 would have been $9.16 trillion instead of $7.64 trillion, and the average income for a family of four would have been $23,440 higher."

THE SIZE AND FUNCTIONS OF
GOVERNMENT AND
ECONOMIC GROWTH

by
James Gwartney
Professor of Economics and Policy Sciences at
Florida State University

Robert Lawson
Assistant Professor of Economics at
Capital University in Columbus, Ohio

Randall Holcombe
DeVoe Moore Professor of Economics at
Florida State University

Prepared for the
Joint Economic Committee

According to the authors, "there is **overwhelming evidence** that both the **size of government and its expansion** have **exerted a negative impact** on economic growth during the last several decades. As government outlays in the United States have grown from 28.4 percent of GDP in 1960 to 34.6 percent in 1996, investment as a share of GDP, labor productivity and real GDP growth have fallen."

Swartney J, Lawson R, Holcombe R. The Size and Functions of Government and Economic Growth. The Joint Economic Committee. http://www.house.gov/jec/growth/function/function.pdf. Accessed 8/8/09

Gwartney et al. examined data on the average year-to-year growth rate of GDP according to the size of government as a share of GDP. The following graph clearly illustrates an inverse relationship between the year-to-year growth of GDP and the size of government in OECD countries.

THE SIZE AND FUNCTIONS OF GOVERNMENT AND ECONOMIC GROWTH

by

James Gwartney
Professor of Economics and Policy Sciences at Florida State University

Robert Lawson
Assistant Professor of Economics at Capital University in Columbus, Ohio

Randall Holcombe
DeVoe Moore Professor of Economics at Florida State University

Prepared for the
Joint Economic Committee

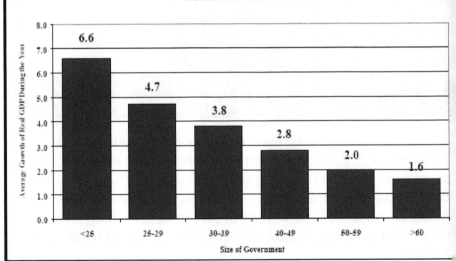

Exhibit 4: Size of Government and the Annual Growth of Real GDP for OECD Countries: 1960-1996

(1)Gwartney J, Lawson R, Holcombe R. The Size and Functions of Government and Economic Growth. The Joint Economic Committee. http://www.house.gov/jec/growth/function/function.pdf. Accessed 8/8/09

President Obama calls increasing government spending an "investment in our future" and claims it will increase prosperity. **The data CLEARLY demonstrate that INCREASING government spending DECREASES prosperity.**

GDP / Capita vs. Gov Spending as % of GDP (GS/GDP) and Tax Revenue as % of GDP (TR/GDP)

This graph compares five of the world's largest economies (based on GDP output per citizen). It shows that the United States has the highest GDP/Capita at $48,000 with a government spending level of 36% of GDP (2008). Conversely, France has the highest government spending level of 52% of GDP and the lowest GDP/Capita at $32,700.

A clear inverse relationship exists!

(1) CIA World Fact Book, https://www.cia.gov/library/publications/the-world-factbook/, accessed 3/10/09
(2) OECD, Member Country Data, http://www.oecd.org/countrieslist/0,3351,en_33873108_33844430
_1_1_1_1_1,00.html,
(3) http://en.wikipedia.org/wiki/List_of_countries_by_GDP_(PPP)_per_capita.
(4) http://knol.google.com/k/alexander-emilfaro/government-spending-and-tax-revenue-as/kpxsjkpzgwux

Government Spending

Bureaucracy, Entitlement Programs and

The biggest threat to our republic is the burden of unsustainable government spending.

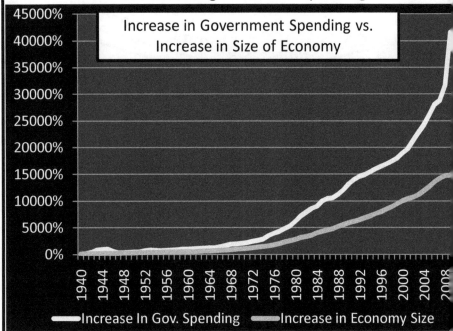

Increase in Government Spending vs. Increase in Size of Economy

⬤ Increase In Gov. Spending   ⬤ Increase in Economy Size

Since the 1940's, America has been the biggest and the fastest growing economy the world has ever known.

Yet over this time, government spending has increased

181% faster than the GDP

(Gross Domestic Product: the measure of economic output of a country).

(1) "U.S. Government Printing Office, http://www.gpoaccess.gov/index.html, accessed 3/12/09
(2) "Highlights of U.S. Federal Budget" various years, Christopher Chantrill, http://www.usgovernment spending.com/budget_gs.php, accessed 3/12/09

for every $\underline{\$15}$ the government spent in 1940,

it will spend $\underline{\$416}$ in 2009

(inflation adjusted)

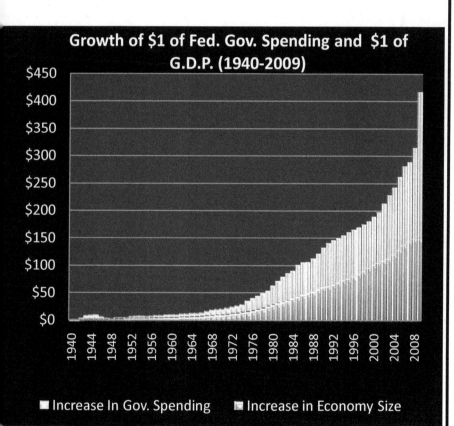

Growth of $1 of Fed. Gov. Spending and $1 of G.D.P. (1940-2009)

■ Increase In Gov. Spending ■ Increase in Economy Size

(1) "U.S. Government Printing Office, http://www.gpoaccess.gov/index.html, accessed 3/12/09
(2) "Highlights of U.S. Federal Budget" various years, Christopher Chantrill,
    http://www.usgovernment
    spending.com/budget_gs.php, accessed 3/12/09

You might like to know...

Fully 69.9% of the federal budget is dedicated to entitlement programs, which are often a redistribution of wealth.

This chart shows how the Federal Government allocated its '08 budget.

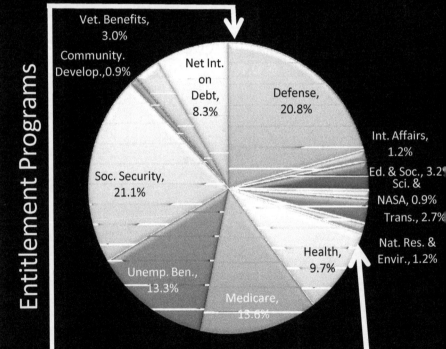

(1) "Outlays by Function and Subfunction, 1962-2013," GPO Access, http://www.gpoaccess.gov /usbudget/fy09/hist.html, accessed 3/14/09

When data was first collected in 1940, payments to individuals (for social welfare programs) cost <u>$17.8 B</u> (adjusted for inflation in year 2000 dollars). The White House's Office of Management and Budget estimates that in 2012, that figure will grow to <u>$1,635.2 B.</u>

Or a 91,000% increase!!!

Increase in Gov. Payments to Individuals (entitlements) vs. Increase as Percent of Total Gov. Spending

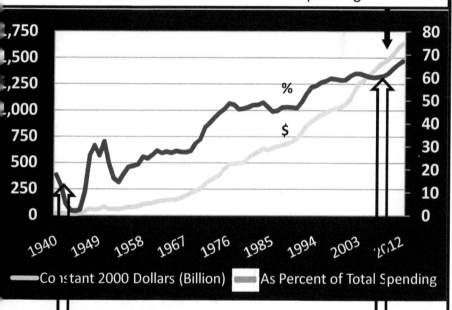

When data was first collected in 1940, payments to individuals (for social welfare programs) accounted for 17.5% of total Government spending.

The White House's Office of Management and Budget Office estimates that in 2012, **payments to individuals will grow to 67% of total spending**.

(1) "Table 11.1—Summary Comparison of Outlays for Payments for Individuals: 1940–2012," Office of Management and Budget http://www.whitehouse.gov/omb/budget/fy2008/hist.html, accessed 4/9/09

The huge increase in government subsidies to individuals is not good for individuals because it decreases growth and creates **dependence!**

The median income (where half earn more and half earn less) grew most when government outlays to individuals grew least!!!!

US Median Income Growth (inflation adjusted, $=2006) **VS.**
US Outlays (entitlements) to Individuals Growth Billions (inflation adjusted, $=2000)

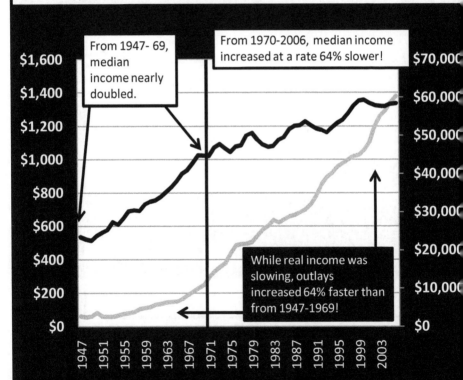

(1) "Table 11.1—Summary Comparison of Outlays for Payments for Individuals: 1940–2012," Office of Management and Budget http://www.whitehouse.gov/omb/budget/fy2008/hist.html, accessed 4/9/09
(2) "Family Income Tables," U.S. Census Bureau, http://www.census.gov/hhes/www/income/histinc/f07ar.html, accessed 4/10/09

The Problem:

This table shows the eight largest social welfare programs and the number of people covered. We will discuss the Tytler Fatal Sequence later (Pg 193), which is applicable because:

Most people who benefit from these programs will never vote for someone who will reduce them, only those who make them bigger (as shown below).

Government Program	Design	Total Covered
Medicaid	Fed. and State partnership that gives health care to children and the poor.	53,400,000.00
Social Security	Provides retirement income to those over 62.	55,000,000.00
Medicare	Provides Health Care to those over 65.	4,200,000.00
Child Nutrition	Gives free school breakfasts and lunches to poor children.	32,300,000.00
Earned Income Tax Credit	Gives the poor money back so they pay a negative tax.	21,200,000.00
Un-Employment	Fed. and State partnership that provides income to those not working.	13,000,000.00
Pel-Grants	Incentive paid for college education.	5,100,000.00
Welfare	Provides cash assistance to the poor.	5,000,000.00

(1) "Federal Entitlements Have Changed," USA Today,
    http://www.usatoday.com/news/washington/2006-03-14-entitle-chart.htm
(2) "FAQ about Social Security," Congress Sandy Levin, http://www.house.gov/levin/levin_issues_
    socialsecurity_faq.shtml, accessed 4/11/09

This cycle of promising more than the other candidate promises was ever apparent in the 2008 presidential campaign. Both Obama and McCain promised a plethora of programs, aid and services to voters in an attempt to buy their votes.

In fact:

... during the second McCain –Obama presidential debate, when a voter questioned both candidates about what they would ask Americans to sacrifice in order to make the country greater, neither could think of a thing.
"Value Driven" – Geoff Colvin, Fortune Magazine 12/8/08

You might like to know...

The following table from Vedder and Gallaway tracks separate components of federal spending over the period of 1947-1997, as a percent of total spending.

Table 3. Components of Federal Spending, 1947-1997,
as Percent of Total

Year	Major Transfer Payments and Income Security	Defense	Net Interest Payments	Other
1947	10.14%	37.10%	12.17%	40.58%
1960	21.48%	52.16%	7.48%	18.87%
1970	29.70%	41.77%	7.36%	21.17%
1980	44.07%	22.68%	8.88%	24.37%
1985	43.96%	26.70%	13.68%	15.66%
1990	44.01%	23.88%	14.70%	14.70%
1996	55.71%	17.03%	15.45%	11.81%

"The types of federal spending growing in relative importance over time – transfer payments [entitlements] or interest on the federal debt – are precisely those programs showing a significant negative relationship to output."

dder RK, Gallaway LE. Government Size and Economic Growth. The Joint Economic Committee.
tp://www.house.gov/jec/growth/govtsize/govtsize.pdf. Accessed 8/10/09

CONGRESSIONAL BUDGET OFFICE

The director of the Congressional Budget Office made an address in September of 2009 where he predicted that the total federal deficit will increase by

300%

of Gross Domestic Product (GDP) as early as 2040.

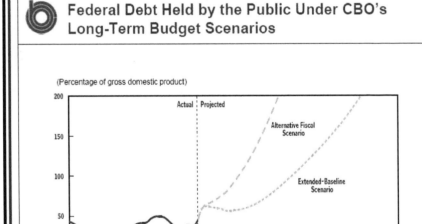

Federal Debt Held by the Public Under CBO's Long-Term Budget Scenarios

(Percentage of gross domestic product)

Actual | Projected

Alternative Fiscal Scenario

Extended-Baseline Scenario

8

(1) "The Budget and Economic Outlook," The Congressional Budget Office, http://www.cbo.gov/f tpdocs/106xx/ doc10624/9.24.09- NationalEconomistsClub.pdf , accessed 10/1/09

"Remember, Democracy never lasts long. It soon wastes, exhausts and murders itself. There has never been a Democracy yet that did not commit Suicide."
- John Adams
April, 1814 in a letter to Thomas Jefferson

This overspending is most certainly the waste that John Adams was talking about.

In fact, <u>the forefathers painstakingly phrased the Constitution to explicitly prevent entitlement spending and the redistribution of wealth</u> ....

The first requisite of a good citizen in this republic of ours is that he should be willing and able to pull his weight.
- Theodore Roosevelt, November 1902

THE CONSTITUTION BEGINS:

We the People of the United States, in order to form a more perfect Union, establish Justice, insure domestic tranquility, provide for the common defence, **promote the General Welfare,** and secure the Blessings of Liberty to ourselves and our Posterity, do ordain and establish this Constitution...

The term **"General Welfare"** has had a changing interpretation over the past 100 years. Before then, great deference was used by governing officials to follow the literal meaning and intent of the founding fathers, which was to allow each man to do what brought him the most happiness so long as it didn't interfere with someone else's happiness.

For political gain, over the last 100 years, both parties have shifted their interpretation widely to be that it is the government's role to facilitate this "Welfare." This liberal interpretation was never the intent of the founding fathers.

Thomas Jefferson,

commenting on the "general Welfare" clause wrote: "To take from one, because it is thought his own industry and that of his father has acquired too much, in order to spare to others who (or whose fathers) have not exercised equal industry and skill, is to violate arbitrarily the first principle of association, "to guarantee to everyone a free exercise of his industry and the fruits acquired by it." (1)

1. "History of the U.S. Tax System," "Fact Sheet: Taxes," United States Department of the Treasury, http://www.treasury.gov/education/fact-sheets/taxes/ustax.shtml, accessed 1/17/09

In fact, Jefferson's interpretation of "General Welfare" was not lost on Grover Cleveland who took a very literal position when, in 1887, a sizeable portion of Texas had suffered from a severe drought. Congress had authorized seeds to be granted to the farmers there to stave hunger, but President Cleveland vetoed the bill.

In a letter to the house on February 16th,1887 he wrote.. And yet I feel obliged to withhold my approval of the plan as proposed by this bill, to indulge a benevolent and charitable sentiment through the appropriation of public funds for that purpose.

I can find no warrant for such an appropriation in the Constitution, and I do not believe that the power and duty of the general government ought to be extended to the relief of individual suffering which is in no manner properly related to the public service or benefit.

The friendliness and charity of our countrymen can always be relied upon to relieve their fellow-citizens in misfortune. This has been repeatedly and quite lately demonstrated. Federal aid in such cases encourages the expectation of paternal care on the part of the government and weakens the sturdiness of our national character, while it prevents the indulgence among our people of that kindly sentiment and conduct which strengthen the bonds of a common brotherhood. (1)(2)

It is amazing how far we've come!

(1) "The Writings and Speeches of Grover Cleveland," by George F. Parker. Cassell Publishing, 1892.
(2) Picture from the Library of Congress, www.loc.gov, accessed 1/20/09

The preceding data on the "optimum" size of government and the growth of the modern welfare state underscores Hayek's famous quote in the Constitution of Liberty:

> *It has been well said that, while we used to suffer from social evils, we now suffer from the remedies for them. The difference is that, while in former times the social evils were gradually disappearing with the growth of wealth, the remedies we have introduced are beginning to threaten the continuance of that growth of wealth on which all future improvement depends.*
>
> F.A. Hayek

"No government voluntarily reduces itself in size. Government programs once launched never disappear."
                          - Ronald Reagan (" A time for Choosing" radio address)

At this ... period, the United States came into existence as a nation, and if their citizens should not be completely free and happy, the fault will be entirely their own.

- George Washington
June 1783

And the increases in entitlement spending and promises only continue.

President Obama has made one of his top initiatives to **create yet another government run health care program.**

To best understand the **dangers** of such a plan, we might first study the fantastic failure of socialism's biggest program in our country:

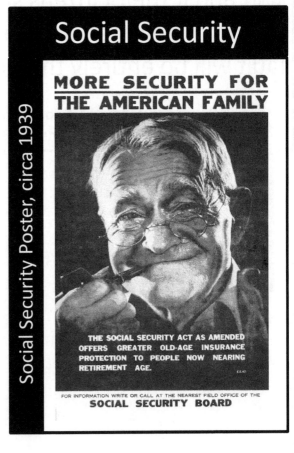

Social Security Poster, circa 1939

Social Security

MORE SECURITY FOR THE AMERICAN FAMILY

THE SOCIAL SECURITY ACT AS AMENDED OFFERS GREATER OLD-AGE INSURANCE PROTECTION TO PEOPLE NOW NEARING RETIREMENT AGE.

FOR INFORMATION WRITE OR CALL AT THE NEAREST FIELD OFFICE OF THE
SOCIAL SECURITY BOARD

(1) "More Security" Poster – 1939, Social Security Administration, www.ssa.gov/history/oldmans.html Accessed 1.20.09

When first rolled out in 1936, the social security tax rate was set at 3% (split evenly between employer and employee) and was scheduled to increase to **no more than a total of 6% by 1949.**

In fact, the government made this promise in its widely distributed 1935 handbook:

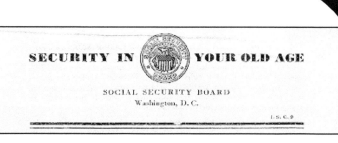

SECURITY IN YOUR OLD AGE

SOCIAL SECURITY BOARD
Washington, D. C.

I. S. C. 9

"...finally, beginning in 1949, twelve years from now, you and your employer will each pay 3 cents on each dollar you earn, up to $3,000 a year. That is the most you will ever pay." (1)

Since that promise <u>the government has grossly underestimated</u> the cost of such an expansive network and over the years has

increased the total Social Security tax to

15.3%.

(1) The 1936 Government Pamphlet on Social Security

Yet despite the 15.3% tax and the 1936 life expectancy:

Figure II.D1. Short-Range OASDI Trust Fund Ratios

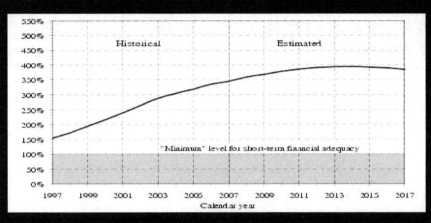

The 2008 OASDI Trustee Report, Section II (Overview), Part D (Projections of Future Financial Status), http://www.ssa.gov/OACT/TR/TR08/trTOC.html, accessed 1/5/09

In **2014,** the Social Security and Disability Trust Fund (which are combined) will peak and declines thereafter. (1)

In **2041,** the trust fund will become exhausted. (1)

These estimates are the most moderate of three that the Trustees use, but based on the Social Security Administration's history we might assume that this is an optimistic figure. Interestingly, "The OASDI 2008 Trustee Report" shows the figures for their "low cost" and "intermediate" modeling but not for their "high cost" model, which would place the date of trust fund exhaustion much earlier.

(1)   The 2008 OASDI Trustees Report Section II (Overview), Part D (Projections of Future Financial Status), http://www.ssa.gov/OACT/TR/TR08/trTOC.html, accessed 1/5/09

To make Social Security permanently solvent it would cost every household ...

if paid today!

(1)   The 2008 OASDI Trustees Report Section II (Overview), Part D (Projections of Future Financial Status), http://www.ssa.gov/OACT/TR/TR08/trTOC.html, accessed 1/5/09

(2)   U.S. Census Bureau, USA Quick Facts , http://quickfacts.census.gov/qfd/states/00000.html, Accessed 1/5/09

How did the Government make such an enormous mistake?

Maybe they didn't!

The Social Security system was designed to never pay the average worker.

"It was designed in 1935 to pay benefits to needy individuals who are

65 years of age or older."

("Compilation of Social Security Laws" Sec. 6. [42 U.S.C. 306] (a))

The life expectancy in 1935 was only 59.2!
("National Vital Statistics Reports, Vol. 56, No. 9, December 28, 2007")

The Historical Ratio of Workers to Retirees

1945 – 42 workers for every 1 recipient

IIIII IIIII IIIII IIIII IIIII IIIII IIIII IIIII III

to

I

2007 – 3.3 workers for every 1 recipient

to

IIII

I

2040 – 2.1 workers for every 1 recipient

to

II

I

(1)

Today, there are **92.2%**

fewer workers for every retiree than there were in 1942.

(1)   The 2008 OASDI Trustees Report Section II (Overview), Part D (Projections of Future Financial Status), http://www.ssa.gov/OACT/TR/TR08/trTOC.html, accessed 1/5/09

Interestingly enough...

"By law, Social Security surpluses must be loaned to the federal government. The federal government is required by law to pay this money back to the Social Security program with interest."

but...

34% of the federal government's 2007 revenue came from Social Security taxes.

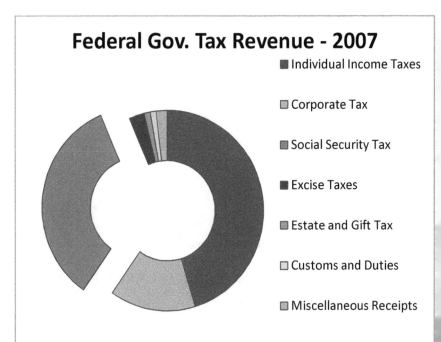

Federal Gov. Tax Revenue - 2007

- Individual Income Taxes
- Corporate Tax
- Social Security Tax
- Excise Taxes
- Estate and Gift Tax
- Customs and Duties
- Miscellaneous Receipts

"Federal Receipts and Collections" – 2007
US Department of the Treasury

And finally, why do we need the government mandated Social Security?

Case Study

A man turns 65 in 2007 and decides to retire. He's worked since the age of 21 and paid the Social Security Tax those years (ranging from 5.4% of his salary to 15.3% between he and his employer). For all of his working years, he earns the exact median income of the country (so exactly half of the population earned more while half earned less).

A total of $143,010

has been contributed in taxes to Social Security and when he takes the benefit he will receive

$1,224/mo

If, instead, he had invested the same amount in the stock market and received the **average** return each year, he would have

$2,226,300 that was all his

and could be annuitized to give an income of

$17,328/mo

How can we fix it? Two options:
To fix the shortfalls of Social Security there are 2 options

1. Increase taxes ... again

To permanently fix the Social Security shortfall it would cost an additional 3.2% in payroll taxes .(1)
The Median Income in 2007 was $50,233(3).This would create an income tax rate of 17.75% (filing singly). Which

means an extra 3.2% is an **18%** increase in income taxes to the average worker.

2. Increase the retirement age

The only other option is to increase the age where full benefits are paid to the increase in life expectancy.

A female born in 1940 is expected to live until 65.7; full benefits are paid at age 65.
A female born in 1955 is expected to live until age 73, or 8 years longer...

Yet the age of full benefit has only increased from 65 to 67

(1) The 2008 OASDI Trustees Report Section II (Overview), Part D (Projections of Future Financial Status), http://www.ssa.gov/OACT/TR/TR08/trTOC.html, accessed 1/5/09
(2) Income, Poverty, and Health Insurance, Proctor, and Jessica C. Smith, U.S. Census Bureau, Current Population Reports, Income, Poverty, and Health Insurance Coverage in the United States: 2007, U.S. Government Printing Office, Washington, DC, 2008
(3) "1040 Instructions, 2008," www.irs.gov, accessed 1/20/09

You might like to know...

Where our country is heading

Socialism, n: (in Marxist theory) the stage following capitalism in the transition of a society to Communism, characterized by the imperfect implementation of collectivist principles.

Collectivism, n: the Socialist principle of control by the state of all means of production of economic activity.

Communism, n:(1) a system of social organization based on holding all property in common, actual ownership being ascribed to the community of the state. (2) ... seeking a violent overthrow of Capitalism ...

PROGRESS

Before President Obama was so measured in his words, he gave the commencement address to Wesleyan University on May 25th of 2008

"But I hope you don't (chase only after the big house and the nice suits and all the other things that our money culture says you should buy)....because you do have an obligation to those who are less fortunate."

" Because our individual salvation depends on **collective salvation**. Because thinking only about yourself, fulfilling your immediate wants and needs, betrays a poverty of ambition."

(1) Random House Webster's College Dictionary, 1999
(2) "Transcript Of Obama's Wesleyan Commencement Address ," Eye Witness News 3 http://www. wfsb.com/news/16389467/detail.html. accessed 3/29/09

Conclusion

The reason for the increase in government spending is largely because candidates run on platforms of bigger promises to more people.

The burden of these programs are not paid with current tax revenue dollars, but instead funded with debt that is pushed off into the future for our generation to shoulder.

This dramatic increase in government spending and entitlement programs has decreased the average earnings growth of the American worker because government spending beyond an "optimum level" decreases economic and wage growth. Our current level of government spending is already well beyond the optimum level, therefore the current level of spending and any future increases in spending and entitlements will contribute to greater slowing in average earnings growth. Entitlement programs also foster dependence and discourage hard work as well as the pursuit of individual advancement because these programs create the idea that "the government should and will provide" and leads to a true "poverty of ambition."

In conclusion, we now know that government spending is increasing at a rate that is unsustainable. There are two reasons why this rate of spending is unsustainable. One, tax payers will be levied with exorbitant taxes to fund these obligations - these tax rates will constrict growth to such an extent that tax revenue will NOT be able to fund the programs. Two, the countries that currently buy our treasury debt (and therefore fund our deficit spending) will STOP purchasing our debt and the programs will come to a screeching halt. The outcome of either scenario is social unrest, likely revolt, and the potential rising of a dictator or strong man to implement societal stability at the expense of our Republic. Sound familiar?

According to the Department of Commerce, Economics and Statistics Administration, between 1980 and 2005, government outlays to individuals (through entitlement, social and welfare programs) increased an incredible 549% , or 210% faster than the economy grew.

Chapter
3
The Consequences of
Taxation

What you need to take away

1. The Founding Fathers were concerned about a central government that was too powerful and originally granted the power of taxation only to the states. (pages 55-58)

2. Since that time, tax revenue per citizen has increased exponentially; 33,970% between 1934 and 2008. (page 61)

3. Income inequality in this country is not increasing. The 1% myth is a tactic used by the left to convince average Americans they are getting slighted and need the government's assistance. (pages 67-70)

4. The Laffer curve shows that tax revenue will start to decrease as tax rates get too high. (page 71)

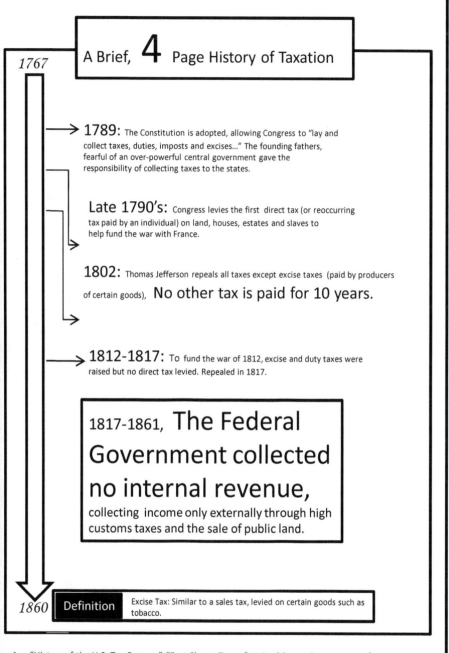

A Brief, **4** Page History of Taxation

1767

1789: The Constitution is adopted, allowing Congress to "lay and collect taxes, duties, imposts and excises..." The founding fathers, fearful of an over-powerful central government gave the responsibility of collecting taxes to the states.

Late 1790's: Congress levies the first direct tax (or reoccurring tax paid by an individual) on land, houses, estates and slaves to help fund the war with France.

1802: Thomas Jefferson repeals all taxes except excise taxes (paid by producers of certain goods), No other tax is paid for 10 years.

1812-1817: To fund the war of 1812, excise and duty taxes were raised but no direct tax levied. Repealed in 1817.

1817-1861, **The Federal Government collected no internal revenue,** collecting income only externally through high customs taxes and the sale of public land.

1860

Definition Excise Tax: Similar to a sales tax, levied on certain goods such as tobacco.

1. "History of the U.S. Tax System," "Fact Sheet: Taxes," United States Department of the Treasury, http://www.treasury.gov/education/fact-sheets/taxes/ustax.shtml, accessed 1/17/09

A Brief, 4 Page History of Taxation

1861

1861 Revenue Act, To pay for the Civil War, the first Income tax was implemented: a flat 3% and not accessed on those earning less than $800.

1862: The first time that tax brackets were used. Incomes up to $10,000 were taxed at 3%: those above were taxed at 5%.

1868-1913: Nearly 90% of federal revenue comes from excise tax.

1872: The income tax is abolished.

1913, The 16th Amendment

gave explicit authority to the Federal Government to impose an income tax without regard to the population of each state (before this, income taxes had to be proportionate to the size of each state).
- Introduced form 1040
- Tax brackets ranged from 1%-7%
- Only accessed on the 1% of population making over $500,000

The **1916** Amendment replaced the term "lawful income" with "income" which gave the government the "right and the need" to know a person or business's economic dealings for the first time, eliminating what had been a private right.
- created estate taxes
- created taxes on "excess" business profits
- raised the maximum tax bracket to 15% (from 7%)

1916

1. "History of the U.S. Tax System," "Fact Sheet: Taxes," United States Department of the Treasury,http://www.treasury.gov/education/fact-sheets/taxes/ustax.shtml, accessed 1/17/09

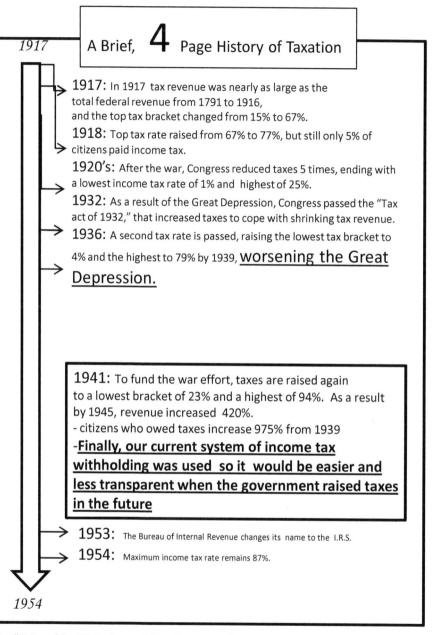

A Brief, **4** Page History of Taxation

1917

1917: In 1917 tax revenue was nearly as large as the total federal revenue from 1791 to 1916, and the top tax bracket changed from 15% to 67%.

1918: Top tax rate raised from 67% to 77%, but still only 5% of citizens paid income tax.

1920's: After the war, Congress reduced taxes 5 times, ending with a lowest income tax rate of 1% and highest of 25%.

1932: As a result of the Great Depression, Congress passed the "Tax act of 1932," that increased taxes to cope with shrinking tax revenue.

1936: A second tax rate is passed, raising the lowest tax bracket to 4% and the highest to 79% by 1939, **worsening the Great Depression.**

1941: To fund the war effort, taxes are raised again to a lowest bracket of 23% and a highest of 94%. As a result by 1945, revenue increased 420%.
- citizens who owed taxes increase 975% from 1939
-**Finally, our current system of income tax withholding was used so it would be easier and less transparent when the government raised taxes in the future**

1953: The Bureau of Internal Revenue changes its name to the I.R.S.

1954: Maximum income tax rate remains 87%.

1954

1. "History of the U.S. Tax System," "Fact Sheet: Taxes," United States Department of the Treasury, http://www.treasury.gov/education/fact-sheets/taxes/ustax.shtml, accessed 1/17/09

A Brief , 4 Page History of Taxation

1981

Reagan's Economic Recovery Tax Act

1981 Due to fiscal and tax policy in the 60's and 70's, high inflation affected the country. To combat it, this act reduced all tax brackets by 25% over 3 years. It also:

. was the first to index rates for inflation

. instituted "accelerated cost recovery," **reducing the disincentive to business to invest in capital goods,** creating increased business development and instituted "marginal" tax brackets .

1986 The 1986 tax reform reduced the highest income tax to 28% (from 50%) and the highest corporate tax to 35% (from 50%). It also created the Alternate Minimum Tax (AMT).

The Clinton Years

1993: After taxes were raised in 1990, Pres. Clinton pushed for a second major increase, pushing the top tax rate to 39.6%.

1997 The "Taxpayer Relief Act" created a "per child" tax credit. This credit allowed for a "negative tax" in some cases meaning that the IRS would send a check even though a filer paid no taxes.

2001: The Bush Tax Cuts

- reduced the top income tax bracket from 39.6 to 33%
- aimed to eventually eliminate the Estate Tax and Gift Tax
- increased the per child tax credit to $1000 from $500

Today

1. "History of the U.S. Tax System," "Fact Sheet: Taxes," United States Department of the Treasury, http://www.treasury.gov/education/fact-sheets/taxes/ustax.shtml, accesse 1/17/09

You might like to know...

The 2% Lie

In his congressional address in late February of 2009, President Obama stated that to fund his aggressive spending plans we would only need to end the tax breaks for the wealthiest 2% of Americans. He goes on to say that if your family earns less than $250K, you will not see you taxes increase "by one single dime."

His plan calls for an increase in income tax on this 2% who make more than $250K from 35% to 39.6%.

The 100% Truth

The Government will spend $4 T in 2010.
According to an article in the Wall Street Journal:

To cover this 2010 spending, a <u>100% income tax</u> would have to be levied on <u>everyone in the country making over $75K</u>.

The truth is that Obama's lax spending will dramatically increase the tax burden on the middle class.

(1) "The 2% Illusion, Take Everything They Earn and it won't be Enough," The Wall Street Journal, 2/27/09
http://online.wsj.com/article_email/SB123561551065378405-IMyQjAxMDI5MzA1NDYwMTQ1Wj.html
accessed 3/24/09

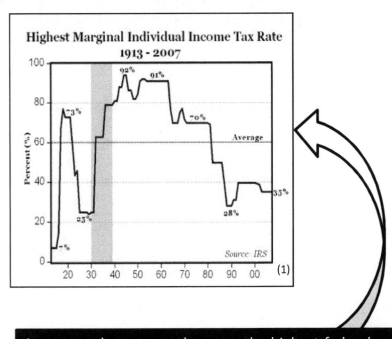

As we now know, over the years the highest federal tax bracket has been nothing less than a remarkable roller coaster ride.

This might lead you to assume that Federal Tax revenue would enjoy the same ride but ...

(1) "Highest Marginal Tax Rates, 1913 – 2008," The Economist Blog, http://www.economistblog.com/2008/03/20/highest-marginal-income-tax-rates-1913-2007/, accessed 1/19/09

The outcome of the tax policy over the last 70 year can be summed up with the graph below. Through these laborious changes, **the tax burden per citizen has increased precipitously.**

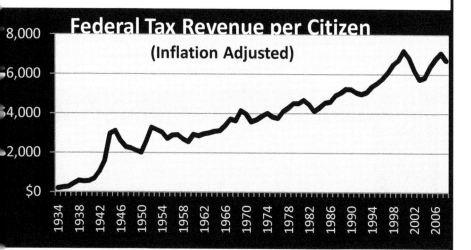

The average U.S. Citizen paid $197 in Federal taxes in 1934 (indexed for inflation at year 2000 dollars).

The average U.S. Citizen paid $6,692 in Federal taxes in 2008 (indexed for inflation at year 2000 dollars).

or, a 33,970% increase!

1 US Census, 1990 "Population, Housing Units, Area Measurements, and Density: 1790 to 1990," TIPSII UPF) GPH21, Census90 8/27/093

2 "Annual Estimates of the Resident Population for the United States…."U.S. Census Bureau, http://www.census.gov/popest/states/NST-ann-est.html, accessed 1/16/09

3 "HS-1. Population 1900-2000," U.S. Census Bureau, Statistical Abstract of the United States

4. "Receipts by Source 1934-2013,"http://www.whitehouse.gov /omb/budget/fy2009/sheets/hist02z1.xls

At the beginning of World War II, tax revenue as a percentage of GDP increased from 5% to 20% and has since been in that general range.

But, because the tax base (GDP) has increased so dramatically, so too has the amount of taxation.

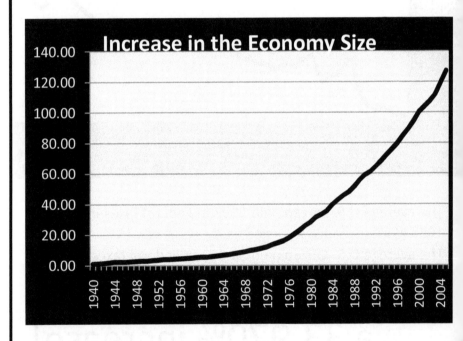

Increase in the Economy Size

While it might seem that the Government has maintained a relatively steady rate of taxation, that same 15%-20% has come from a much larger economy.

The most important point to glean from this chapter is that the Federal government has **an insatiable appetite to spend and to control.**

As the Treasury Department admits:

" Another important feature ... was the return (in 1941) to income tax withholding (where your employer submits taxes from your pay to the IRS). This greatly eased the collection of the tax ...it also greatly reduced the taxpayer's awareness of the amount of tax being collected, i.e. it reduced the transparency of the tax, which made it easier to raise taxes in the future."[1]

Government revenue needs cannot be passed to corporations either. If taxes are coming from corporations, who ends up paying the tax?
It is passed to the consumer through higher prices!

1. "History of the U.S. Tax System," "Fact Sheet: Taxes," United States Department of the Treasury, http://www.treasury.gov/education/fact-sheets/taxes/ustax.shtml, accessed 1/17/09

You might like to know...

Governments spend more money than they take in via taxes. They issue debt to cover this deficit and must pay interest or "service the debt."

President Obama's 2010 budget proposal, "A New Era of Responsibility, Renewing America's Promise," increases the debt held by the public from $5.8 trillion in 2008 to an estimated $15.4 trillion in 11 years or a...

264% increase!

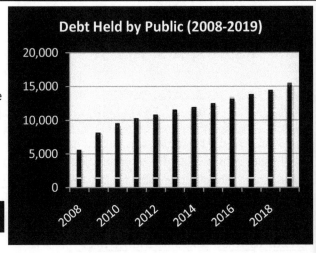

In 2008, the interest owed on the $5.8 Trillion was $243.9 Billion or, <u>8% of the Federal budget</u>, or <u>$1,574 for every worker each year.</u>

If we extrapolate that to 2019, every worker in the U.S. will owe <u>$4,155 every year</u> just to pay the interest on the public dept.

This is $4,155 that should be going toward personal wealth.

(1) "A New Era of Responsibility, Renewing America's Promise," Office of Management and Budget, 2010 Budget, http://www.gpoaccess.gov/usbudget/fy10/pdf/fy10-newera.pdf, accessed 3/14/09
(2) "Outlays by Function and Sub function, 1962-2013," GPO Access, http://www.gpoaccess.gov/usbudget/fy09/hist.html, accessed 3/14/09

Who Pays Taxes?

The <u>top 1%</u> make **22%** of total income and pay ***40%*** of total income taxes.

The <u>top 5%</u> make **37%** of total income and pay ***60%*** of total income taxes.

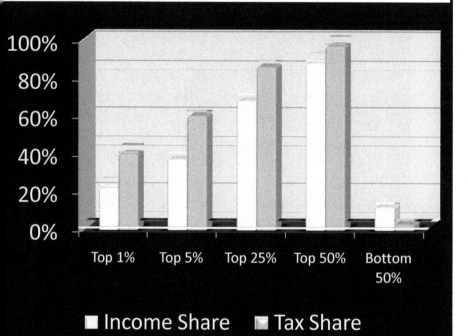

The Current Tax Code is Steeply **PROGRESSIVE!**

It is important to note that 50% of the country already pays almost NO income tax.

1. IRS. Statistics of Income 2008. http://www.irs.gov/pub/irs-soi/08sprbul.pdf. Accessed 4/27/2009.

If someone still thinks extensive government social welfare programs are essential you might say;

I don't believe I should have to pay for these programs, but If you feel that the government should be in charge of these

why not send them a check to fund it?

Send your check to:
Bureau of the Public Debt
Department G.,
Washington D.C. 20239-0601

They will even let you choose what program you want to fund.

That is, of course, unless you mean everyone else should pay, not you.

Of course no one will cut a check. This is because liberals propose to pay for their programs with other people's $$$.

The 1% Myth

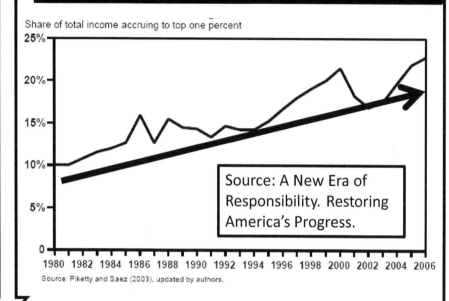

Liberal Argument:
In America, the rich get richer and the poor get poorer!

Share of total income accruing to top one percent

Source: A New Era of Responsibility. Restoring America's Progress.

Source: Piketty and Saez (2003), updated by authors.

The above chart, produced by Thomas Piketty and Emmanuel Saez, demonstrates that over the last 25 years, the share of income going to the top 1% has consistently increased and therefore, the share going to everybody else has gotten smaller.

According to liberals, this data is justification to support increased taxes on the wealthy, more expansive government redistribution of wealth, and increased government interference in the private market to correct this **INJUSTICE**.
- **Unfortunately this MYTH is predicated on invalid methods for calculating wage inequality.**
- **These statistics are produced solely from federal income tax return data and *don't account for three major factors*, that when corrected, CANCEL OUT this growing trend in income disparity.**

First, according to Alan Reynolds, a senior fellow at the Cato Institute, "studies based on tax return data provide highly misleading comparisons of changes to the U.S. income distribution because of *dramatic changes in tax rules and tax reporting in recent decades.*"

Top Tax Rates: 1979

Highest marginal individual income tax rate was **70%**

Corporate tax rates were **46%** on income above $100,000

Since the early 1980's, individual tax rates have been reduced multiple times and this has led to a shift from reporting business income on corporate returns to individual returns by filing as S-corporations.

Top Tax Rates: 2007

Highest marginal Individual income tax rate was **35%**

Corporate tax rates were **39%** on income between $100,000 and $335,000 and reduced rates below that level

Increases in top income levels are the result of BOOKKEEPING CHANGES in the way business and individual incomes are reported!

(1) Reynolds, Alan. "Has U.S. Income Inequality *Really* Increased?" The Cato Institute. January 8, 2007. 19 Apr 2009. http://www.cato.org/pub_display.php?pub_id=6880

Income ratio of the Top 1% equals:

$$\frac{\text{Income of Top 1\% (Numerator)}}{\text{Total Income of Everyone (Denominator)}}$$

Shifting between corporate and individual income tax return filing FALSELY ELEVATES the numerator causing FALSE INCREASES in income inequality.

In addition, there are two major factors in the Piketty/Saez data which FALSELY DEPRESS the denominator. These factors also lead to FALSE INCREASES in income inequality.

NUMBER ONE

In recent years, an increasingly large share of middle-income investment returns have been sheltered inside tax-favored accounts, such as 401(k)s and IRAs which are NOT recorded on income tax returns.

NUMBER TWO

Over the last 25 years there has been a LARGE growth in transfer payments for low-income families. This income is excluded from the Piketty/Saez tax-return data highlighted by President Obama.

(1) Reynolds, Alan. "Has U.S. Income Inequality *Really* Increased?" The Cato Institute. January 8, 2007. 19 Apr 2009. http://www.cato.org/pub_display.php?pub_id=6880

The HEART of the liberal agenda depends on **SELLING A LIE...**

That increasing government spending will lead to:
Growth – Opportunity – Prosperity

Therefore, they need this distraction - the 1% MYTH – to convince people they're victims and need MORE government.

You know better:
Don't let liberals propagate the 1% MYTH!

Conclusion

Despite the radical shifts in overall taxation through the years, it's actually in the Government's interest to keep taxes low in order to receive more tax revenue.

This idea is explained by the famous "Laffer" Curve, an old economic concept sketched on a napkin by Arthur Laffer in a meeting in 1984:

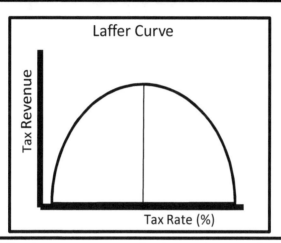

Laffer Curve

Tax Revenue

Tax Rate (%)

Definition

Briefly, the curve suggests that increasing taxes from a very low level will increase government revenue. It also holds that at some point an increase in taxes will actually reduce government revenue, because it will decrease the incentive to work. At the far right of the curve (100% taxation), there will be no revenue because there will be no incentive to work. (1)

In 1980, if you earned $500,000 you would owe $330,074 of income taxes (not including sales, state, local, property taxes….). (1)

Where was the incentive to work?

If you earned $500,000 in 2008, you would owe $153,596 in income taxes.

(1) "U.S. Federal Individual Income Tax Rates History, 1913-2009," The Tax Foundation, http://www.taxfoundation.org/taxdata/show/151.html, accessed 3/24/09

Chapter
4
The Threat of
Government Run
Health Care

What you need to take away

1. There have always been about the same percentage of uninsured people living in our country even as Government health care coverage has greatly increased. (page 75)

2. The WHO rankings that rank the U.S . 37th in overall health care are very biased. (page 78-84)

3. The United States performs better than socialized health care systems on well-documented disease specific outcomes. (page 86)

Why would we ask the same government that has so mismanaged social security to run

Government-run Health Care ?

One of the major themes of Obama's 2008 presidential campaign was to offer more government-run health care options.

Advocates of such a system will usually cite three major arguments:

1. There are 45 million uninsured living in the United States.
2. Our health care system is not ranked highly.
3. Socialized systems like the ones that exist in Canada, France and the UK provide better care and cost less.

Let's research each point.

(1) Embassy of the United States, Oslo, Norway

In 2007 there were 45.6 million uninsured people in the U.S. or …

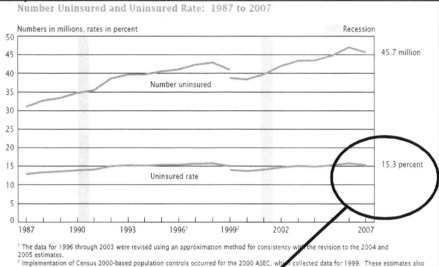

Number Uninsured and Uninsured Rate: 1987 to 2007

Numbers in millions, rates in percent

Recession

45.7 million

Number uninsured

15.3 percent

Uninsured rate

1987   1990   1993   1996¹   1999²   2002   2007

¹ The data for 1996 through 2003 were revised using an approximation method for consistency with the revision to the 2004 and 2005 estimates.
² Implementation of Census 2000-based population controls occurred for the 2000 ASEC, which collected data for 1999. These estimates also reflect the results of follow-up verification questions that were asked of people who responded "no" to all questions about specific types of health insurance coverage in order to verify whether they were actually uninsured. This change increased the number and percentage of people covered by health insurance, bringing the CPS more in line with estimates from other national surveys.
Note: Respondents were not asked detailed health insurance questions before the 1988 CPS. For information on recessions, see Appendix A.
Source: U.S. Census Bureau, Current Population Survey, 1988 to 2008 Annual Social and Economic Supplements.

Notice that the rate of the uninsured has fluctuated within a very narrow band over the last 20 years

15.3 % of the total population

(1) DeNavas-Walt, Carmen, Bernadette D. Proctor, and Jessica C. Smith,U.S. Census Bureau, Current Population Reports, P60-235 *Income, Poverty, and Health Insurance Coverage in the United States: 2007,*U.S. Government Printing Office, Washington, DC,2008

And who are these uninsured?

Of the 45.6 million uninsured people living in our country:

8.1 million (17%)are under the age of 18 and 7.8 million (18%) are in a household with someone 18 or younger, (1) and probably already eligible for Medicaid.

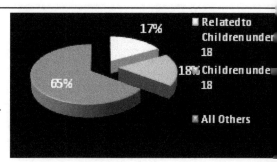

8.4 million (19%) make between $50K and $75K and 9.1 million (20%) make over $75K a year. (1)

The median income in 2007 was $50,233. (2)

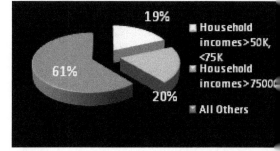

And 9.7 million (21%) are not citizens or are illegal immigrants. (1)

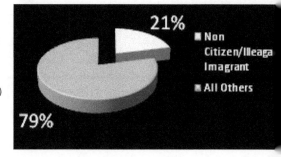

(1) "People Without Health Insurance Coverage by Selected Characteristics: 2006 and 2007" U.S. Census Bureau, Current Population Survey, 2007 and 2008 Annual Social and Economic Supplements., table 6
(2) "Social Security and Medicare Tax Rates" , SocialSecurity.gov - accessed 12/21/08 , Social Security Online - Trust Fund Data

SO...

of the 15.3% of our country who are uninsured, a <u>much smaller percentage</u> (4-8%) are incapable of procuring their own coverage.

We now know that the majority have an income that is at least 480% higher than the 2008 poverty level, (1) are already eligible for a government health care program, or are not a citizen of this country.

But what if someone argues that our health care is not as good as socialized systems?

(1) The United States Department of Health and Human Services
http://aspe.hhs.gov/poverty/08Poverty.shtml - Accessed 1/1/09

Argument 2: Our Health Care system is not ranked highly.

Critics of our health care system argue that the health care system in our country does not rank as highly as the Socialized Systems of Canada, France or the UK.

They are most likely quoting the <u>World Health Organization's</u> report called:

"MEASURING OVERALL HEALTH SYSTEM PERFORMANCE FOR 191 COUNTRIES"

which was produced in 2000 and quoted by Michael Moore in his movie "Sicko."

This report ranks "the overall efficiency" <u>(not benefit)</u> as follows: (1)

1. France
18. United Kingdom
20. Sweden
32. Canada
<u>37. United States</u>

Those who cite the WHO rankings typically present them as an objective measure of the relative performance of national health care systems.

THEY ARE NOT!

(1) "Measuring overall health system performance for 191 countries," Table 1, World Health Organization, 2000

You might like to know...

Who is W.H.O.?

"WHO is the directing and coordinating authority for health within the United Nations system. **It is responsible for providing leadership on global health matters**, shaping the health research agenda (and) setting norms and standards..." (1)

The World Health Organization (as shown above), is given the authority to have "leadership on global health matters." But unfortunately, W.H.O. <u>also</u> has a political agenda.

Case Study
On 12/26/08, the Palestinians ended a 6 month cease fire by launching over 300 missiles into Israel without warning, to which Israel responded with military force.

<u>On their website, W.H.O. stated</u>
"WHO calls for an immediate end to hostilities in the Gaza Strip and urges Israel to ensure immediate provision of fuel and critical life-saving/trauma care supplies." (1)

(1) "About WHO," http://www.who.int/about/en/, accessed 1/10/09
(2) WHO warns of rise in deaths, human suffering in Gaza, 12/31/09, www.who.int/en, accessed 1/6/08

We can't expect any such ranking to be perfect, but the W.H.O's political bias carries over strongly into this report.

In fact, of the 36 countries that rank higher than the U.S.:

- **89%** have some form of Socialized health care and

- an average **71.3%** of total health care spending comes from their Government (2)

(The U.S. Government accounted for 45.5% of overall spending in 2007 (3)

W.H.O. Formula Weight for Overall Ranking

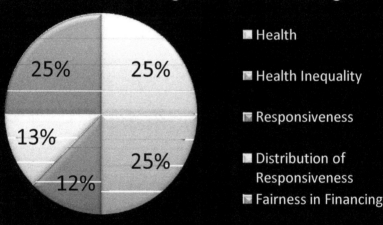

- Health
- Health Inequality
- Responsiveness
- Distribution of Responsiveness
- Fairness in Financing

Let's look at each one of these variables.

(1) Whitman G. WHO's Fooling Who? The World Health Organization's Problematic Ranking of HealthCare Systems. Cato Briefing Papers. No. 101. 2008
(2) World Health Organization, WHO Statistical Information System, "Core Health Indicators, 2004/05," www.who.int/en, accessed 1/10/09
(3) National Center for Health Statistics Health, United States, 2007 With Chart book on Trends in the Health of Americans, Hyattsville, MD: 2007 Table 121. Gross domestic product, federal, and state and local government expenditures, national health and average annual percent change: United States, selected years 1960-05

Defined Below are the Five Variables that W.H.O. Use:[1]

1. Health Level – 25%   *– a reasonable measure*

Health level is a direct measure of the health of a country's residents, so its inclusion is fair.
· Measures a country's disability-adjusted life expectancy (DALE)
· Can be affected by a wide variety of factors other than the health care system, such as poverty, geography, homicide rate, typical diet, tobacco use and so on.

2. Responsiveness – 12.5%   *– a reasonable measure*

Measures a variety of health care system features, including service, protection of privacy, choice of doctors and quality of amenities.
These features represent aspects of the quality of health care services, so there is a strong case for including them.

> The U.S. was ranked **#1** in
> # Responsiveness!

3. Financial Fairness – 25%   *– an un-reasonable measure*

Measured by determining a household's contribution to health expenditure as a percentage of household income (beyond subsistence), then looks at the dispersion of this percentage over all households.

The wider the dispersion in the percentage of household income spent on health care, the worse a nation will perform on the FF factor and the overall index.

Financial fairness is not an objective measure of health attainment, but rather reflects a value judgment that rich people should pay more for health care, even if they consume the same amount.

(1) Whitman G. WHO's Fooling Who? The World Health Organization's Problematic Ranking of Health Care Systems. Cato Briefing Papers. No. 101. 2008.

4. Health Distribution – 25%   *- an un-reasonable measure*

Measures inequality in health care level within a country.

5. Responsiveness Distribution –   *- an un-reasonable measure*

Measures inequality in health care responsiveness within a country.

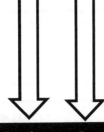

Why are they un-reasonable?

According to Greg Whitman of the Cato Institute: "It is entirely possible to have a health care system characterized by both extensive inequality *and* good care for everyone." Suppose, for instance, that:

Country A has health responsiveness that is "excellent" for most citizens but merely "good" for some disadvantaged groups, while,

Country B has responsiveness that is uniformly "poor" for everyone.

Country B would score *higher than Country A in terms of responsiveness* distribution, despite Country A having better responsiveness than Country B for even its worst-off citizens. The same point applies to the distribution of health care level.

(1) Whitman G. WHO's Fooling Who? The World Health Organization's Problematic Ranking of Health Care Systems. Cato Briefing Papers. No. 101. 2008.

Finally, even if you can accept the shortfalls of the formula and outcome...

By W.H.O.'s own admission

the information used to come to these conclusions are poor.

"For the purposes of this analysis, the weights used in the construction of the composite index have been used consistently, i.e., without considering uncertainty in the valuations of the different components."

"It is important to note that, by using health expenditure as the health system input to the production of health outcomes, the interpretation of overall efficiency differs significantly to the interpretation of efficiency from many existing ... studies."

"The **80% uncertainty intervals on the overall efficiency index** reflect the estimated distribution of the efficiency index derived from these 1000 different regressions." (1)

Definition

Uncertainty Intervals (or confidence intervals) are usually measured to a 95% range (which means that 19 of 20 tests produce the same outcome). An interval of 80% is considered "wide," meaning more information should be gathered on the sample.(2)

1) World Health Organization, WHO Statistical Information System, "Core Health Indicators, 2004/05," www.who.int/en, accessed 1/10/09
2) Wikipedia Online Encyclopedia, www.widipedia.com, accessed 1/10/09

You might like to know...

The W.H.O. rankings are based on statistics constructed in part from random samples. As a result, each rank has a margin of error.

Using the overall attainment (OA) ranking, the U.S. rank could range anywhere from 7 to 24. By comparison, France could range from 3 to 11 and Canada from 4 to 14. (1)

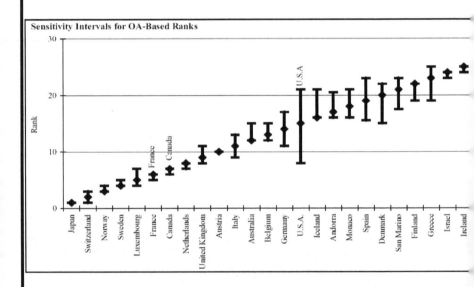

Sensitivity Intervals for OA-Based Ranks

One cannot say with great confidence that the United States does not do better in the OA ranking than France, Canada, the UK and most other countries.

(1) Whitman G. WHO's Fooling Who? The World Health Organization's Problematic Ranking of Health Care Systems. Cato Briefing Papers. No. 101. 2008.

Because of the uncertainty of the W.H.O. report, Statistics Canada and the CDC

commissioned an intergovernmental health report called:

Joint Canada/United States Survey of Health, 2002-03

This Report compared the privatized health care of the United States with the single payer (all expenses paid by the Government) socialized health care system of Canada.

Percentage Privately Paid vs. Publicly Paid Health Care Costs

United States

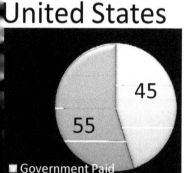

Canada

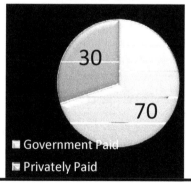

(1) World Health Organization, WHO Statistical Information System, "Core Health Indicators, 2004/05," www.who.int/en, accessed 1/10/09

(2) National Center for Health Statistics Health, United States, 2007
With Chart book on Trends in the Health of Americans, Hyattsville, MD: 2007
Table 121. Gross domestic product, federal, and state and local government expenditures, national health and average annual percent change: United States, selected years 1960-05

Joint Canada/United States Survey of Health, 2002-03

The Study provided interesting insight into these two significantly different health care systems:

"Overall, most Canadians (88%) and Americans (85%) reported being in good, very good, or excellent health. More Americans reported being ... in excellent health (26%) and in fair and poor health (15%) — compared with Canadians (24% and 12%, respectively)."

"Women in the U.S. reported that they were in excellent health (25% vs. 23%)."

"American women aged 50-69 were more likely to have had a mammogram within the last 2 years compared with Canadian women of the same age (82% vs. 74%)."

"Americans were more likely to be 'very satisfied' with their health care services (both all services and doctor services) while Canadians were more likely to be 'somewhat satisfied' (for all services)."

(1) Joint Canada/United State Survey of Health, 2002-03, Statistics Canada, Center for Disease Control and Prevention, Statistics Canada Catalogue 82m0022-XIE

You might like to know...

Of the <u>940,000</u> medical doctors in the United States, <u>243,000</u> are graduates of foreign medical schools. (1)

"There are 12,040 Canadian-educated physicians living in the United States." (2)

"The migration of US-trained physicians to work in Canada, only 400-500 physicians, is miniscule in comparison." (2)

A system that attracts **24** more physicians for every **1** that leaves is a superior system for the physician . <u>Does that mean it is a superior system for the patient?</u>

(1) AMA Physician Masterfile, American Medical Association, http://www.ama-assn.org/ama/pub/categor/2673.html, accessed 1/11/09
(2) "The Canadian contribution to the US physician workforce," The Canadian Medical Association, Robert L. Phillips, Jr, Stephen Petterson, George E. Fryer, Jr and Walter Rosser, http://www.cmaj.ca/cgi/content/full/176/8/1083, accessed 1/11/09

Government health care leads to the rationing of care.

Countries that utilize socialized health care systems spend less than the U.S. because they ration care through a variety of mechanisms. One mechanism is to restrict access to new and more expensive technologies such as new medical devices and therapies, which improve the practice of medicine for all members of society.

Canada's "Health Canada" and the United Kingdom's "Department of Health" already engage in the rationing of care to the detriment of their citizens. The rationing is dictated by a government board that uses a formula to determine when a procedure can and can not be performed and if a life saving drug is too expensive.

DO NOT BELIEVE that this same rationing couldn't happen in America because it ALREADY does. The president has created the "Comparative Effectiveness Research Council" which is intended to ration care for the rest of us.

On June 16th, Fox News interviewed Georgia Congressman Tom Price, a surgeon, who commented on the rationing. If you "YouTube" the congressman you will find the startling video clip.

(1) Image Citation, "Congressman Tom Price" http://tom.house.gov/, Accessed 12/31/09

The **Problem** with Government Health Care

Socialized medicine restricts patient access to health care services and **sets the fees** for which health care providers can be reimbursed for their services!

Socialized systems can NOT provide patients lower costs and more services than a free market health care system.

Here are a few recent cases from Canada:

Friendly neighbors, rationed health care

Case 1: A female with headaches and vision loss and **a brain tumor identified on MRI was told she would have to wait months for further specialty care even though her vision was deteriorating.** Instead, she went to the Mayo Clinic in Arizona and paid for her surgery.

Case 2: A 57 year old Alberta man was told he **was "too old"** to receive a hip resurfacing surgery for his arthritic hip. He was also told he couldn't pay with his own money to have the procedure done in Canada. (1)

In 2008, a sampling of Canadian citizens waited a <u>median of 121 days</u> from mandatory general-practitioner referrals to treatment. (1)

In the US, the average time to see a specialist is 20.5 days (2)

(1) Esmail Nadeem, "Too old for hip surgery." The Wall Street Journal. February 9, 2009. http://online.wsj.com/article/SB123413701032661445.html. Accessed 2/9/09

(2) Erin Thompson, "Wait Times to See Doctors are Getting Longer," USA Today, http://www.usatoday.com/news/health/2009-06-03-waittimes_N.htm, accessed 9/12/09

Socialized Health Care CASE STUDY

An Associated Press story on February 4th, 2009 tells of a Japanese man who, while riding his bicycle, was hit by a motorcycle.

Citing a lack of equipment, specialists, beds and staff, **14 hospitals refused to admit him,** and he died on the scene while in the ambulance.

According to the article, "More than 14,000 emergency patients were rejected at least three times by Japanese hospitals before getting treatment in 2007."

The government study that the article cites shows that the worst case was a woman in her 70's with respiratory problems was rejected 49 times in Tokyo. (1)

The Japanese Government Funds 82% of all care in Japan(2)

Socialized Health Care CASE STUDY

Dr. Olle Stendahl, professor of medicine at Linkoping University in Sweden, lamented to Swedish daily newspaper *Dagens Nyheter* last year:

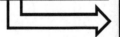

"In our budget-governed health care system there is no room for medical professionals to challenge established views. New knowledge is not attractive, but typically considered a problem that brings increased costs and disturbances in today's slimmed-down health care system." (3)

The Swedish government funds 82% of care in Sweden.(2)

(1) "Injured Japanese man Dies After 14 Hospitals Refuse to Admit Him," Associated Press Fox News, http://www.foxnews.com/story/0,2933,487747,00.html, accessed 2/4/09
(2) "Core Health Indicators, World Health Organization," http://www.who.int/ whosis /database/ core/core_select_process .cfm?country =jpn&ind icators=nha, accessed 2/09
(3). Larson SR., Lessons from Sweden's Universal Health System: Tales from the Health-care Crypt ,2008, Journal of American Physicians and Surgeons, http://www.jpands.org/vol13no1/larson.pdf, accessed 9/12/09

The __Problem__ with Government Health Care

Because socialized medicine sets provider fees (lower than insurance companies do in a more privatized system) and restricts patient access to health care, especially new and more expensive services, it discourages private and public investment in research and development.

This may be why....

50% → of new drugs developed over the last 20 years were created in the United States (the most privatized HC system of any Industrialized country). (1)

72% → of the last 25 winners of the Nobel Prize in Medicine are either U.S. citizens or individuals working here. (1)

(1) Tanner, Michael D. "The Grass Is Not Always Greener: A Look at National Health Care Systems Around the World." The Cato Institute. March 18, 2008. 9 Feb 2009 http://www.cato.org/pub_display.php? pub_id=9272

You might like to know...

How about the Big Drug companies?

A Free market with great reward will best drive innovation

- For every 10,000 compounds investigated, only five are ever tested as potential medicines in a clinical trial.
- Only one in five is ever approved for patient use.
- Only three out of ten approved for patient use generate revenues that meet or exceed average research and development costs.
- The average R&D cost per drug approved by the FDA is $802 million. It takes an average of 12-15 years to develop a new drug.

For every 100 drugs that go to clinical trial, only 6 will be profitable!

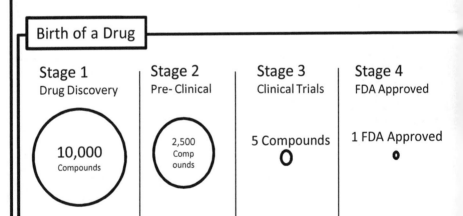

Birth of a Drug

Stage 1 Drug Discovery	Stage 2 Pre-Clinical	Stage 3 Clinical Trials	Stage 4 FDA Approved
10,000 Compounds	2,500 Compounds	5 Compounds O	1 FDA Approved o

14 Years

(1) "What Goes into the Costs of Prescription Drugs," Phrma, 2004, http://www.phrma.org/files/ Cost_of_Prescription_Drugs.pdf, accessed 3/21/09

Chapter
5
Solutions to the
Health Care
Problem

The Problem with Government Run Health Care
And Free Market Solutions
(to reduce cost and expand access)

1. One of the fundamental problems with our healthcare system is the way healthcare is paid through a third party and not directly by the patient. (pages 96 and 97)

2. Across the globe, health care spending is rising at a rapid rate – not just in the US. (pages 98 and 99)

3. Roadmap for real healthcare reform: There are at least four solutions outside of increasing government spending, that can cut costs and expand access to care. (pages 102-114)

Understanding the Cause of Health Care Inflation

This is one of those cases in which the imagination is baffled by the facts.

Adam Smith

The problem with health care in the United States is that it *costs too much* and everyone agrees that something has to be done to fix it.

In a policy review prepared for the Commonwealth Foundation Laffer, Arduin and Winegarden describe how the government's involvement in the health care system has resulted in:

"[A] large and growing health care wedge – an economic separation of effort from reward, of consumers (patients) from producers (health care providers), caused by government policies...The wedge is a primary driver in rising health care costs, i.e., inflation in medical costs."

Most of the energy of political work is devoted to correcting the effects of mismanagement of government.

Milton Friedman

THE PROGNOSIS FOR NATIONAL HEALTH INSURANCE: A PENNSYLVANIA PERSPECTIVE. Laffer A, Arduin D and Winegarden W. http://www.commonwealthfoundation.org/doclib/20090831_LafferFull.pdf. Accessed 8/11/09

Before the government got involved in the medical field, health care was regarded as a product to be traded voluntarily in a free market. Medical providers competed to provide the best quality services at the lowest possible prices and almost all Americans could afford basic health care and those who could not were able to rely on abundant private charity.

The private sector funded over three quarters of the country's health care expenditures, individuals paid nearly one-half of total costs out-of-pocket and health care inflation was in-line with the consumer price index (CPI).

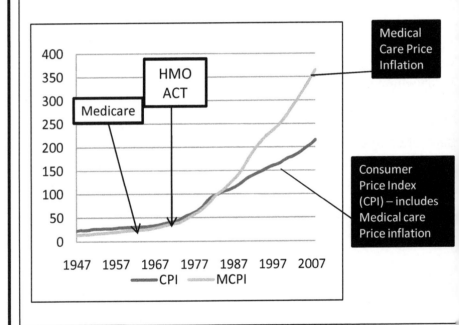

The passage of **Medicare** in 1965 and the **HMO Act** of 1973 fundamentally changed the way health care was purchased. As the government began to cover a growing percentage of health care costs and insert more regulation over the health care market, total out-of-pocket expenditures fell. Today, out-of-pocket expenses account for *only one-tenth* of total health care spending.

The creation of **Medicare** in 1965 made individual insurance for those over age 55 obsolete. This legislation provided *subsidized, unrestricted* health care for seniors and led to a frenzy of spending by patients and doctors.

The **HMO Act** of 1973 provided *grants and loans to start or expand* a Health Maintenance Organization (HMO), and required employers with 25 or more employees to offer federally certified HMO options, which were cheaper than those in the individual market due to the generous government subsidies.

These two pieces of legislation had the calamitous effect of shifting costs from the consumer to a third party and created the "wedge" between patients (consumers) and doctors (health care suppliers).

When a third party pays the cost of routine health care services, consumers become insensitive to prices, quality and choice of care setting. Individuals respond to lower cost-sharing (more comprehensive coverage) by utilizing more care, as well as more expensive care because they do not face the full price of their decisions at the point of utilization.

Insurance is a tool for mitigating financial risk.

But when it comes to health care - and *only* health care - we don't use it for that purpose. Instead, we misuse insurance through the collective, resource-pooling mechanism of group comprehensive insurance used to pay for a routine cost of living that should be part of everyone's monthly budget.

There's little difference between this broken dynamic and "spreading the wealth around" when one examines the details of the economics involved. *This was exactly the intention of the legislation described above.*

It must also be noted that healthcare costs are rising as a percentage of gross domestic product (GDP) all over the world – *not just the United States*. The following figure represents data from Hagist and Kotlikoff who studied the growth in healthcare spending for 10 developed countries over the time period 1970 – 2002 and projected government healthcare spending over the next 50 years.

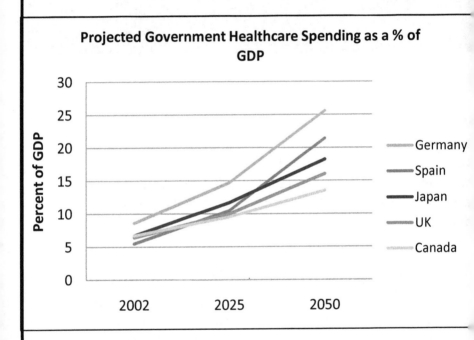

The authors found that "Government health care expenditures have grown much more rapidly than the economy in all developed countries. Between 1970 and 2002, these expenditures per capita grew at almost twice the rate of gross domestic product (GDP) per capita in 10 countries studied: Australia, Austria, Canada, Germany, Japan, Norway, Spain, Sweden, the United Kingdom and the United States."

Hagist C, Kotlikoff LJ. Health Care Spending: What the Future Will Look Like. NCPA Policy Repo No. 286. June 2006. ISBN #1-56808-158-8.

Healthcare inflation is skyrocketing around the globe as a result of government run "comprehensive" healthcare policies.

Other countries that provide "comprehensive" government-run health care coverage to their citizens only spend less, relative to the US, because these other contries limit access to the most expensive health care services and are tort adverse.

Therefore, health care reform policies that seek to either:

1. Increase government run healthcare programs or

2. Subsidize the purchase of private "comprehensive" healthcare coverage

Health care reform will *only exacerbate health care inflation*. They will not be able to control costs without rationing services or significantly increasing taxes and will likely utilize both mechanisms.

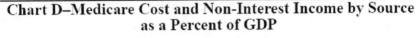

Proponents of government run health care cite Medicare as a model that demonstrates how government run health care is more efficient and effective than the private market

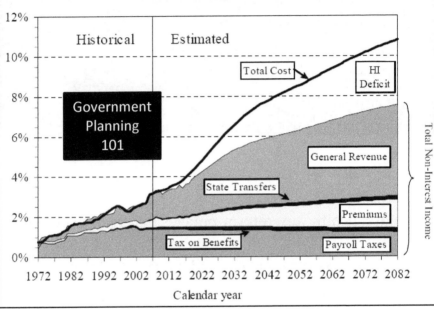

Chart D–Medicare Cost and Non-Interest Income by Source as a Percent of GDP

Historical | Estimated

Government Planning 101

Total Cost

HI Deficit

General Revenue

State Transfers

Premiums

Tax on Benefits

Payroll Taxes

Total Non-Interest Income

1972 1982 1992 2002 2012 2022 2032 2042 2052 2062 2072 2082
Calendar year

President Obama's health care reform agenda includes a government provided "public option" to control costs and make health care affordable. He claims it won't require continuous tax subsidies. Then he cites Medicare as a model for reform – yet the data from the Medicare Advisory Board demonstrates that *Medicare has required general fund revenues (tax subsidies) almost since its inception to operate, and the necessity for those funds is only projected to keep increasing.* If someone tries to argue with you that the government's plan will control costs and be self-sustaining *tell them you have some ocean front property in Arizona to sell to them.*

A Summary of the 2009 Annual Reports. Social Security and Medicare Boards of Trustees. http://www.ssa.gov/OACT/TRSUM/index.html. Accessed 8/20/2009.

The state of Massachusetts provides a case study in which it predicts what is likely to happen if the administration creates a new government-subsidized insurance plan. In 2006, Massachusetts passed sweeping healthcare legislation which included the creation of a new government subsidized insurance plan called Commonwealth Care.

The plan was projected to cost taxpayers $725 million per year however, by 2008 the cost had risen to $869 million, representing a *20% increase* over the projected yearly costs!

The goal was to increase competition in the private market in order to decrease premium costs, or as President Obama would say, "Keep private insurance companies honest."

The unintended consequence - *the one you can typically expect with government intervention* - was exactly the opposite! Insurance premiums rose by 7.4% in 2007, 8-12% in 2008 and are expected to rise 9% this year. By comparison, nationwide insurance costs rose by 6.1% in 2007, 4.7% in 2008 and are projected to increase 6.4% this year.

1) Tanner M. Massachusetts Miracle or Massachusetts Miserable. CATO Briefing Papers No. 12. http://www.cato.org/pubs/bp/bp112.pdf. Accessed 5/25/2009.

ROADMAP FOR REAL HEALTH CARE REFORM

We must begin with the recognition that:

Health care services are products to be traded voluntarily in a free market.

<u>and</u>

Insurance is a tool for mitigating risk.

Individuals should receive their full employment compensation including the current compensation being paid into their health insurance benefits.

Government should allocate employment-based tax deductions to individuals to purchase health care services on an open market just like individuals and families shop for individual single and family plans at the current time.

- If individuals face the full cost of their premiums and health care purchases they will shop for the highest quality care at the lowest cost and exert downward pressure on the market.

Individual ownership of health insurance policies will provide security for individuals if they change or lose their job.

Under the current tax code, individuals who purchase health insurance through their employer do it with <u>pre-tax dollars.</u>

CASE STUDY

This means that an individual <u>with</u> employer-sponsored health care could have 40K in income and a 10K health care policy, making their total compensation $50K a year.

However, another individual <u>without</u> employer-sponsored health care could earn the same total compensation of $50K and need to purchase a 10K health care policy.

This second person would pay extra federal, state, local, social security and FICA taxes on $50K instead of $40K.

This is clearly NOT fair and makes it more difficult for individuals without employer-sponsored coverage to purchase insurance. Less tangibly, it encourages workers to demand comprehensive third-party coverage because any medical care purchased through their employer plan is effectively tax-free.

2nd Solution	Give every individual or business the ability to purchase insurance in a national market, from insurance companies in any state.

The general public and media are mostly unaware that state legislatures have a significant impact on the cost of health insurance premiums in the small group and individual health insurance markets. Because regulations vary from state to state, the cost of health insurance premiums can differ widely depending on the state where one lives. A sampling of state-mandated services (some ridiculous) include: acupuncture, breast reduction, contraceptives, dieticians, drug abuse treatment, hair prosthesis, in vitro fertilization, massage therapy, etc. While all these services have individual value they should NOT be compulsory benefits that individuals interested in purchasing medical insurance should be burdened with. They exist because special interest groups have successfully lobbied politicians to cover them.(1)

For more information on the rules and regulations that effect you, visit your state insurance commissioner's website.

A simple solution to cut costs and expand access <u>overnight</u> would be to allow consumers to purchase health insurance across state lines. This would decrease the cost of available insurance options and have the added benefit of increasing competition within the private insurance industry where a few insurers typically dominate a state market. This also allows for the natural cost efficiencies of a free market through competition.

1) Health Insurance: Overview and Economic Impact in the States.
http://www.ahipresearch.org/PDFs/StateData/StateDataFullReport.pdf. accessed 8/08/09.

The following figure was composed of data from the 2007 America's Health Insurance Plan's (AHIP) report titled, "Health Insurance: Overview and Economic Impact in the States." The figure is a random compilation of average health care premiums among states for their individual single and family markets.

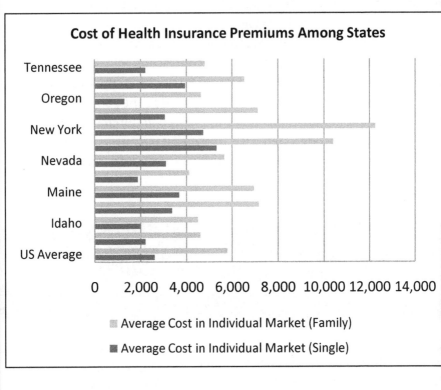

Cost of Health Insurance Premiums Among States

- Average Cost in Individual Market (Family)
- Average Cost in Individual Market (Single)

Premiums vary widely from state to state as a result of existing regulations. The government's job is to enforce voluntary contracts between individuals and insurers; it has no right to demand what insurers must provide and individuals must purchase.

Health Insurance: Overview and Economic Impact in the States.
http://www.ahipresearch.org/PDFs/StateData/StateDataFullReport.pdf. accessed 8/08/09.

The cost of heath insurance across the country varies widely for the same policy from the same insurer (in this case United Health Group's Co-Pay Saver $2500). These quotes are for a family of four in average health who have a $2500 deductible for major procedures and a low co-pay for other services (i.e.. $35 for prescription drugs).

(1) UnitedHealthOne Quote Generator, www.goldenrulehealth.com accessed 8/11/09

The same exact coverage from the same company costs <u>40%</u> more in Amarillo TX than it does in Philadelphia!!

As noted earlier, there are several variables contributing to the difference in cost across state lines and even within states (as seen between Clearwater FL and Miami FL) not least of which are the intrusive regulations put in place by state and local governments.

3rd	Allow the purchase of basic health insurance with low premiums and high deductibles that covers major illness or injury, in conjunction with tax-free accounts for out-of-pocket expenses, including deductibles.
Solution	

Data from the Kaiser Family Foundation suggests that the premium savings that come from switching to high-deductible coverage (HDHP) can be considerable. In 2005, the average employer-provided health plan cost $4,024 for self-only coverage and $10,880 for family coverage. The average annual premium for an HSA-compatible HDHP was $2,700 for self-only coverage and $7,909 for family coverage.

> The difference in premiums was **$1,324** for individuals and **$2,791** for families.

After two years, the premium savings alone could more than cover the average annual deductible. Therefore, HSAs would allow healthy people to save money that they are currently "throwing down the premium hole," while still maintaining protection against large medical bills. [1]

CASE STUDY

If a 25 year old puts $1,324 into an HSA every year and receives 8% interest they would have

$416,897

that would be available to use for medical expenses when he or she will statistically use it most. If it isn't used, these assets will pass to beneficiaries!

(1) Cannon M. *Health Savings Accounts Do the Critics Have a Point?* Cato Policy Analysis No. 569. May 2006.

Consumer Driven Health Care Saves Money And Controls Cost!

The 2007 United Benefits Advisors (UBA) health-plan survey, the largest survey of health plans in the country, recently reviewed more than 16,000 health plans and found that: *Low-premium, high-deductible premiums grew less than 3% in 2006, compared to all other plans, with an average premium increase of more than 7%!*

CIGNA Health Care conducted a two-year study of 430,000 of its members with consumer-driven and HMO/PPO plans. For the first year of the study, medical costs for members with consumer plans were more than 12% lower than those for HMO and PPO members. *Members with HSA-eligible plans also increased their preventive care and use of maintenance medications for chronic conditions, and their expenses still decreased!*

nst DM. 2008: Next steps for health savings accounts. *Health Policy Prescriptions* 2008:6 No.1

You might like to know...

The Whole Foods health care story is a template for how instituting the kind of reforms advocated for in this chapter can drive down health care costs and make insurance available for the majority of those who currently can't afford it.

John Mackey, the CEO of Whole Foods, was quoted in the Wall Street Journal saying, "[combining] our high deductible plan (patients pay for the first $2,500 of medical expenses) with personal wellness accounts or health savings accounts works extremely well for us." [1]

> -The plans' premiums plus other costs come to $2,100 per employee, and about $7,000 for a family (half of what other companies pay).

Further proof that implementing consumer-driven health care reform policies will drive down health care costs.

Moore S. The Conscience of a Capitalist. *The Wall Street Journal*. 10/3/09.

4th Solution — Pursue Aggressive Tort Reform to Decrease Defensive Medicine Costs.

The final link in the chain

The common law of torts, awards damages to a patient when his or her doctor acts negligently and causes an injury.

Although the direct costs of lawsuits and settlements account for a very small fraction of total health spending, **less than 1%,**

the costs of defensive medicine are far greater!

Defensive medicine is medical practice based on fear of legal liability rather than on patients' best interests.

Defensive medicine accounts for 200-500 billion dollars worth of health care spending annually.

Direct reforms to reduce the costs of liability include caps on damages and abolition of punitive or exemplary damages.

Restrictions on contingent and conditional

fees will also cause the number of lawsuits to fall. Although historically prohibited by common law, the USA now allows lawyers' fees to depend on the outcomes of their cases. Empirical research suggests that restrictions on contingent fees generally lead to the elimination of the weakest claims.

There is no denying that some defensive medicine practices are being driven by frivolous lawsuits and these practices are driving up health care spending and inflation.

Defensive medicine is medical practice based on fear of legal liability rather than on patients' best interests. It has been driven to absurd levels in America by the threat of frivolous lawsuits. This has resulted in ballooning medical expenditures.

One study in JAMA from Studdert et al., of 824 high-risk specialist physicians in a volatile malpractice environment, found that **93%** reported practicing defensive medicine. "Assurance behavior" such as ordering tests, performing diagnostic procedures and referring patients for consultation, were very common (92%).

An authoritative study from the Massachusetts Medical Society found that **83%** of physicians surveyed reported practicing defensive medicine. ***One quarter*** of all CT scans, MRIs, Ultrasounds and specialty referrals were ordered for defensive reasons. This number is astounding, and *if we extrapolate it to total healthcare spending we're looking at close to 500 billion dollars annually!*

A more conservative estimate from The Pacific Research Institute puts the costs of defensive medicine at ***more than 200 billion dollars annually.***

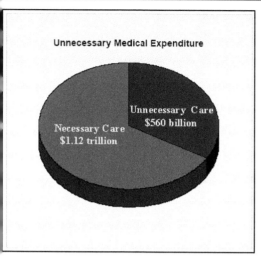

Unnecessary Medical Expenditure

Unnecessary Care
$560 billion

Necessary Care
$1.12 trillion

Defensive medicine may account for as much as **$200 - $500 Billion** dollars worth of unnecessary medical expenses every year!

(1)

Research shows that reforms that directly reduce the costs of liability have the greatest effect on limiting defensive medicine practices.

Kessler and McClellan used longitudinal data for almost all elderly patients admitted to a hospital with serious cardiac illness, matched with information on the existence of tort reforms from the US in which the patient was treated. They reported that *reforms that directly limited liability, such as caps on damages, reduced hospital expenditures by 5-9% in the late 1980's and led to NO important differences in mortality or serious complications.* (2)

(1) http://cdhc.ncpa.org/learn/facts-and-figures. Accessed 1/5/09
(2) Kessler DP, McClellan MB. *Do doctors practice defensive medicine? QJ Econ* 1996: 111:353-390

You might like to know...

When President Obama addressed the American Medical Association on June 15th, 2009 to gain their support for his health care plan he said:

"I want to be honest with you. I'm not advocating caps on malpractice awards, which I personally believe can be unfair to people who've been wrongfully harmed."

How can anyone find the best solution to a problem if they refuse to examine all of the options?

(1) Image, www.healthreform.gov, accessed 8/16/09

Chapter
6
History of
Financial
Crises

What you need to take away

1. Government interference in the free markets through bailout and stimulus have never worked.

2. The Great Depression is an excellent case study of this point. (page 133-139)

3. There are two major economic philosophies at work today. (pages 125-130)

What Caused the Financial Crisis
in 2 Pages

1.

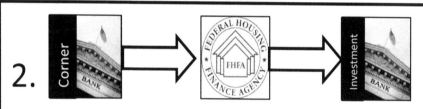

Lending to unqualified home buyers increased demand and raised home values. This lending was the result of: 1. lax underwriting by banks, and 2. government encouragement (see next case study).

2.

Instead of holding the mortgages, the originating bank would "sell" the mortgage to another bank or Freddie Mac or Fannie Mae, who in turn would sell these assets to investment banks.

3.

The investment banks would bundle many mortgages together creating "mortgage backed securities," slicing them up and making them available to individual investors marketed as conservative, income producing investments.

[1] "The Financial Crisis of 2008," Encyclopedia Britannica,. http://www.britannica.com/EBchecked/topic/1484261/global-financial-crisis, accessed 2/18/09

What Caused the Financial Crisis
in 2 Pages

To further persuade investors, insurance companies began to guarantee these bundled mortgages with "credit default swaps" (if the mortgages lost value, the insurance company was on the hook).

4.

- These swaps were quickly traded by speculators hoping to cash in on the "secure" investments.
- In 2001 there were $900 billion insured by swaps, by 2008 there were $62 trillion.

5.

Because of the stimulated lending practices (see step 1) some home owners were not able to pay their mortgages (sometimes a result of adjustable rate mortgages). These home owners were forced to sell their homes, increasing supply and significantly driving down home values.

6. The reduction in home values reduced <u>the value of the mortgage backed securities</u> (see step 3) who then called in their insurance protection (credit default swaps, see step 4). This put unsustainable pressure on financial giants like AIG who, because of leverage, could never fully insure these swaps.

7.Finally, because of a lack of confidence between lenders (individual and corporate) and financial institutions, lending (or credit) slowed at a fantastic pace.

(1) "The Financial Crisis of 2008," Encyclopedia Britannica,. http://www.britannica.com/EBchecked/topic/1484261/global-financial-crisis, accessed 2/18/09

You might like to know...

Over the last 18 years, homeowners missing mortgage payments bottomed in 2005 at 1.44% and today, at 9.8%, are now at their highest levels

or a 580% increase!

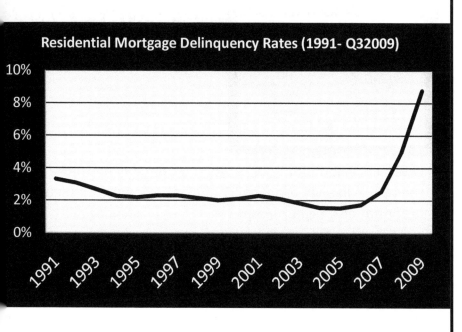

Residential Mortgage Delinquency Rates (1991- Q32009)

Leaving 91.2% of homeowners making on-time payments.

(1) "Delinquency Rates, All Banks," Federal Reserve Statistical Release, http://www.federal reserve.gov/Releases/chargeoff/delallsa.htm, accessed 3/3/09

You might like to know...

Q. How can things "be this bad" if
<u>91.2%</u> of homeowners are
paying their mortgage on time?

A. Leverage.

Leverage, a common tool, is when a company has more than $1 of liability for each $1 of asset, allowing for higher profit but also higher losses.

With regard to the financial crisis, many banks were leveraging their "mortgage backed securities" by 30:1, or more!

This means that for every 1% of homeowners not paying their mortgage, the holders of the "mortgage backed securities" or "credit default swaps" suffer up to a

30% loss.

Case Study

The housing crisis, which is the root of the overall financial crisis, is the result of plunging home values. These values were inflated for two main reasons:

1. Lax lending standards, and
2. The misconception that housing was a fail - safe investment. (1)

These potent elements paired to cause an unprecedented rise in home values.

rom 1963 to
heir peak in
006, median
ome values
ncreased

157%

aster than
flation.

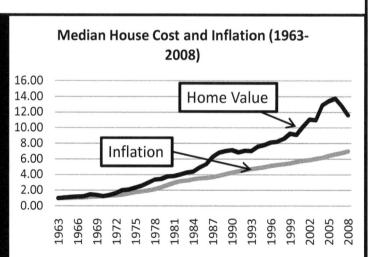

Median House Cost and Inflation (1963-2008)

Home Value

Inflation

16.00
14.00
12.00
10.00
8.00
6.00
4.00
2.00
0.00

1963 1966 1969 1972 1975 1978 1981 1984 1987 1990 1993 1996 1999 2002 2005 2008

(1) "Housing Crisis," Peter Coy, Business Week, 1/31/08
(2) "Median and Average Sales Prices of New Homes Sold in United States," U.S. Census Bureau, http://www.census.gov/const/uspricemon.pdf, accessed 2/15/09

The lax lending standards that helped create this crisis were the fault of:

- The government
(for interfering with the natural development of the free markets by artificially creating demand for homes by giving access to credit to borrowers who otherwise should not have had it)

- The banks and borrowers
(for failing to address the mortgage holders capacity to pay)

In 1977, Congress passed the "Community Reinvestment Act" that mandated all F.D.I.C. insured banks give more loans to lower income households (or less credit worthy borrowers). The act was significantly broadened by Clinton in 1993.

Bill Clinton as quoted in his memoir "My Life."

"One of the most effective things we did was to reform the regulations governing financial institutions under the 1977 Community Reinvestment act. The law required federally insured lenders to make an extra effort to give loans to low and modest income borrowers ... After the changes we made between 1993-2000, banks would offer more than $800 billion in (loans) to borrowers covered by the law. A staggering figure that amounted to well over 90% all loans made in the 23 years of (the act)." (1)

(1) "My Life," Bill Clinton, Vintage Books New York, Pg. 68
http://photos.state.gov/libraries/usinfo/4110/week_3/122007
bill-200.jpg

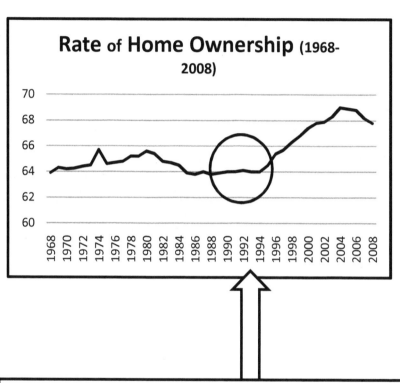

Rate of Home Ownership (1968-2008)

Before the Community Investment Act was amended in 1993, the rate of home ownership had long hovered near 64%. You might argue that it was this amendment that caused the significant increase in demand that artificially drove up the value of homes, nudging us towards the current housing crisis.

(1) "Housing Vacancies and Home Ownership," US Census Bureau, http://www.census.gov/hhes/www/housing/hvs/qtr408/q408tab5.html accessed 2/14/09

Case Study

How is the government responding?

Within the stimulus bill, signed by President Obama in February of 2009, the tax incentive to purchase a house was significantly increased.

The incentive had been a $7,500 tax credit given to first time home buyers that would have to be paid back over 10 years, effectively amounting to a interest free loan.

The new incentive is a $8,000 tax break, available to ALL home buyers, and does not need to be paid back. (1)

Once again the Government has wrongfully interfered with the free markets.

"We can't solve problems by using the same kind of thinking we used when we created them."

- Albert Einstein

(1) "Senate's Tax Credit Favors Higher-Income Homebuyers," Ryan J. Donmoyer, Bloomberg.com, http://www.bloomberg.com/ apps/news?pid=20601087&sid=a30KUnGy1VEM&refer=home accessed 2/15/09

Where Do We Go From Here?

The laws of economics, which we've already discussed at length still apply ... *even during recessions*.

There are two major economic philosophies at work in America today.

Both are briefly explained next. By gaining a basic understanding of each, you will be at a fundamental advantage over most of your contemporaries.

John Maynard Keynes - Keynesian Economics

Background:
Born in England on June 5th, 1883.
Studied politics and economics at Cambridge.
Earned M.A. in 1909 and returned to Cambridge to teach economics.
Scored lowest in economics when he took the Civil Service exam; "I evidently knew more about economics than my examiners" he quipped.
Attended Versailles Peace Conference post-WWI as economic advisor.

Work:
After the Versailles Conference, Keynes wrote "The Economic Consequences of the Peace" which accurately predicted that Germany would not be able to pay reparations and would threaten all of Europe. His approach was implemented post-WWII to prevent a similar situation.

"The General Theory of Employment, Interest and Money," written in 1936, is by far Keynes' most important work, in which he theorized that the key to solving high unemployment was government employment programs.

Theory

Economic followers of Keynes (or Keynesians) believe that the key to solving high unemployment is to increase government spending and to run a budget deficit. Keynesian economics was strongly embraced by FDR during the great depression and (because it promotes government intervention in the free markets) is increasingly being cited as the only solution to our current financial crisis by some progressives.

(1) Encyclopedia Britannica,
http://www.britannica.com/EBchecked/topic/315921/John-Maynard-Keynes, accessed 2/9/09
(2) "John Maynard Keynes," Robert Reich, Time Magazine online,
www.time.com/time/time100/scientist/profile/keynes03.html, accessed 2/9/09
(3) Picture Citation, www.liberalhistory.org.uk/uploads/keynes.jpg, accessed 2/9/09

When anyone advocates <u>Keynesian Economics,</u>
consider this:

When Keynes released the German Language version of
"The General Theory of Employment, Interest and
Money" in Nazi Germany in 1936, he prefaced the book
with:

"Nevertheless the theory of output as a whole... is much more easily adapted to the conditions of a <u>totalitarian</u> state, than is the theory of production and distribution of a given output produced under conditions of free competition..." (1)

Totalitarianism:
A form of government that seeks to dissolve individual liberties and control all aspects of individual life through coercion and repression.
Examples of this single party, empowered central government are Nazi Germany under Hitler (1933-45), the Soviet Union under Stalin (1924-53), and Italy under Mussolini (1922-43). (2)

(1) Encyclopedia Britannica, http://www.britannica.com/EBchecked/topic/315921/John-Maynard-Keynes, accessed 2/9/09
(2) Encyclopedia Britannica, http://www.britannica.com/EBchecked/topic/600435/totalitarianism, accessed 2/9/09

Milton Freidman — Monetarist Economic Philosophy

Background:
Born in New York City in 1912.
Graduated from Rutgers in 1932 with a degree in
   mathematics and economics.
Earned Masters ('33) and PhD ('46) from U. of
Chicago where he would teach for 30 years.
A social liberal, he was an economic advisor to
Nixon and Reagan.
Nobel Economics Laureate 1976.

Work:
Best known as the founder of <u>Monetarism</u> which hypothesized that the
   money supply was most important variable in the economy.
In 1957, <u>"A Theory of Consumption Function"</u> described his important
   idea that a household's spending and saving is related to permanent
   income instead of temporary or one time incomes or events.
In 1963 he co-authored <u>"A Monetary History of the U.S. (1867-1960)"</u>
where he claimed that the Great Depression would have been a usual
downturn if not for the missteps taken by the federal reserve.

Theory

Friedman demonstrated that Keynesian economic policy leads to
stagflation (the combination of low growth and high inflation).
Friedman formulated an alternative macroeconomic policy to
Keynesianism called Monetarism, which argues that the
government cannot micromanage the economy because business
owners, investors and consumers will realize what the government
is doing and shift their behavior – this reaction is known as ***rational
expectations.***

(1) Encyclopedia Britannica, http://www.britannica.com/EBchecked/topic/220152/
   Milton-Friedman2/9/09
(2) "Milton Freidman, Economist as Public Intellect," Robert Formaini, Dallas Fed Reserve,
   http://www.dallasfed.org/research/ei/ei0202.html, accessed 2/9/09
(3) Picture Citation, www.loc.gov/rr/business/images/friedman-180_uc.jpg, accessed 2/9/

In Friedman's "Consumption Function Theory," he proposed that businesses, investors and consumers only spend what they interpret to be permanent income (like a raise in pay or permanent tax reduction) and save what they interpret to be temporary income (like government rebates or temporary tax reduction).

Friedman's Monetarism (or **rational expectations**) in a simplified sense is like *the law of gravity* – what goes up, must come down; likewise, what money the government spends today must be paid for by higher taxes tomorrow.

How about the 2008 tax rebates?

Many economists don't believe the $168 billion mailed to tax payers last spring was effective. To counter that impression, the National Retail Federation has circulated its own statistical analysis of what people did with the first $110 billion of rebates. According to this analysis, only $42 billion or **38%** of the $110 billion was spent, the rest was used to bolster savings or pay debt.

If most of the money was saved (62%) or used to pay existing debt, the stimulus checks did not work very cost-effectively to bolster the economy, in which growth can only be attained by spending. So why did the government issue the stimulus? Look forward to Alexander Tytler's argument (page 192):

"the majority always votes for the candidate who promises the most benefits from the public treasury"

Rather than stimulating the economy, politicians were instead buying votes with money they are **borrowing from our generation!**

(1) "How Obama will Stroke the Economy," Business Week, 11/24/08

Rational expectations is an assumption used in many contemporary or *new Keynesian* macroeconomic models. In a recent paper, Cogan et al. used the Smets-Wouters model to evaluate the effects of the most recent stimulus plan – The American Recovery and Reinvestment Act. The Smets-Wouters model is representative of current thinking in macroeconomics using "new Keynesian" models.

Crowding Out of Private Consumption and Investment in the February 2009 Stimulus Legislation

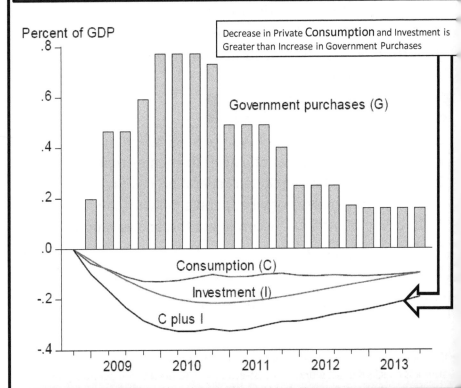

In the Smets-Wouters model there is a strong crowding out of private investment. Hence, ***both consumption and investment decline as a share of GDP*** in the first year. The declines in consumption plus investment are greater than the increases in government spending. According to the authors, ***the impact on GDP is negative for many years beyond 2013.***

1. Cogan JF, Cwik T, Taylor JB, and wieland V. New Keynesian versus Old Keynesian Spending Multiplie http://www.volkerwieland.com/docs/CCTW%20Mar%202.pdf. Accessed 3/20/09

The best way to stimulate the economy, *even during recessions*, is through **cuts in government spending!**

In a major study appearing in the *American Journal of Economics*, Alberto Alesina of Harvard found that the best way to make an economy grow is to cut government spending while the best way to usher a decline is to increase taxation. The researchers studied econometric data for 18 large OECD member countries to assess the effects of government spending and taxation on investment.

Table 15: Fiscal adjustments: Fiscal policy and macroeconomic indicators.

	Expansionary				Contractionary			
	Bef.	Dur.	Aft.	Aft.-Bef	Bef.	Dur.	Aft.	Aft.-Bef.
Primary Spending	42.96	41.71	41.36	-1.60 *	40.32	40.24	40.15	-0.17
	(1.43)	(1.42)	(1.35)		(1.36)	(1.37)	(1.40)	
Total Revenue	40.10	41.42	41.57	1.47 *	36.97	39.03	39.65	2.69 *
	(1.45)	(1.43)	(1.41)		(1.48)	(1.51)	(1.58)	
GDP Growth rate deviation from G7	-0.79	-0.45	-0.19	0.60	0.82	-1.12	-0.86	-1.68 *
	(0.24)	(0.33)	(0.31)		(0.40)	(0.44)	(0.28)	
GDP Growth rate	1.31	2.65	3.41	2.10 *	3.73	1.34	1.91	-1.82 *
	(0.24)	(0.30)	(0.30)		(0.27)	(0.24)	(0.27)	
Δ Priv.Consumption	1.16	2.30	3.03	1.87 *	3.76	1.19	1.84	-1.93
	(0.36)	(0.38)	(0.30)		(0.55)	(0.45)	(0.31)	
Δ Bus.Investment	-0.36	3.49	5.24	5.60 *	4.59	-0.39	0.29	-4.30 *
	(0.99)	(1.24)	(1.13)		(1.22)	(1.60)	(1.31)	

"Primary spending" represents total government spending as a share of GDP and "total revenue" represents government tax revenue as a share of GDP. Each of the indices has a value to represent the level before, during and after the expansion or contraction and the change in the indices is represented as "Aft-Bef".

Economic growth is implemented by spending cuts while economic decline is implemented by increased taxation – *most importantly*, these trends hold even for large fiscal expansions and contractions. <u>A review of large fiscal contractions in the past only highlights Alesina's conclusions.</u>

The "financial crisis" currently gripping our economy is encouraging many liberals and conservatives to argue for far-reaching government intervention.

To best understand the current banking and housing crisis and the shortcomings of government intervention we might benefit from a brief history of the Great Depression.

Great Depression

1929

→ **October 29, 1929.** Black Tuesday and the crash of the stock market, marking the beginning of the "Great Depression." It is caused by an unbalanced economy, large discrepancies in opportunity, an immature banking system, but perhaps most of all the dramatic economic increases of the 1920's and the belief that America would benefit from perpetual prosperity which was called the "New Era."

→ **January 1932. The Reconstruction Finance Corp. (RFC)** is begun by President Hoover to lend federal funds to private financial institutions: the idea is that recovery could "trickle down."

→ **March 4, 1933.** Franklin D. Roosevelt is elected with a 61% majority and the **"New Deal"** begins the next day with the **"Emergency Banking Act"** extending Gov. assistance to strong banks and reorganizing weak ones.

May 1933. Agricultural Adjustment Admin. (AAA) is created and pays farmers to restrict production and to burn 10 million acres of cotton and bury 9 million lbs of pork.

1933

(1) "The American Journey, A History of the United State," Goldfield, Abbott, Anderson, Argersinger, Argersinger, Barney, Weir, Prentice Hall Press, 2001, New Jersey.

Great Depression

1933, The First 100 Days

National Recovery Admin. (NRA) created to encourage industrial growth by suspending antitrust laws, among others. **Federal Emergency Relief Act (FERA)** provides assistance to the unemployed and creates government funded jobs. **Civilian Conservation Corp. (CCC)** combines work relief with conservation. **Public Works Admin. and Civil Works Admin.** create work relief for large public projects and public works. **Tennessee Valley Authority (TVA)**, develops power generation.

1934: The **Securities and Exchange Commission (SEC)** is created to regulate stock market.

1935: The **National Recovery Admin.** is declared unconstitutional. The **Wagner Labor Relations Act** encourages unionization. **Social Security Admin.** is created. The **Banking Act** increases Federal control over banking system. The **Revenue Act** creates tax brackets, estate taxes and raises corporate taxes. **Resettlement Admin.** created to aid dislocated farmers. **Rural Electrification Admin.** provides electricity to rural areas. **Emergency Relief Act** creates more emergency public jobs. **Workers Progress Admin.** begun to aid the unemployed and create jobs.

1937: The **Farm Security Admin.** is created to loan money to small farmers to buy rehabilitated farms.

1937

(1) "The American Journey, A History of the United State," Goldfield, Abbott, Anderson, Argersinger, Argersinger, Barney, Weir, Prentice Hall Press, 2001, New Jersey

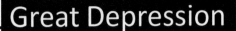

Great Depression

→1938:
The **Fair Labor Standards Act** established maximum hours and minimum wage.

Maybe it is less important to know each of these programs and more important to know that between 1932 and 1938:

15 <u>new</u> government administrations were created.

(1) "The American Journey, A History of the United State," Goldfield, Abbott, Anderson, Argersinger, Argersinger, Barney, Weir, Prentice Hall Press, 2001, New Jersey

And the results of these 15 new government offices?

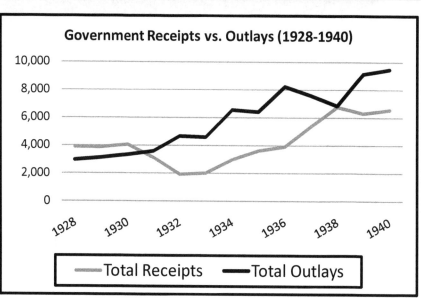

Government Receipts vs. Outlays (1928-1940)

Legend: — Total Receipts — Total Outlays

Federal Tax Revenue increased by **68%** and

Government Spending increased by **220%**.

While there had been a budget surplus in years prior, the federal deficit from 1932-1940 was **24,000,000,000** or 3.7 times 1940 total revenue.

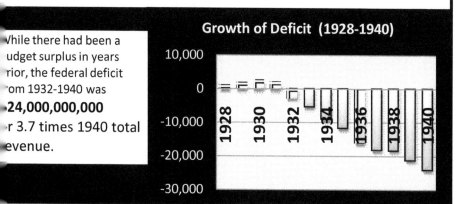

Growth of Deficit (1928-1940)

(1) Office of manager of Budget "Receipts by Source"1783-2013,"http://www.gpoaccess.gov/usbudget/fy07/hist.html

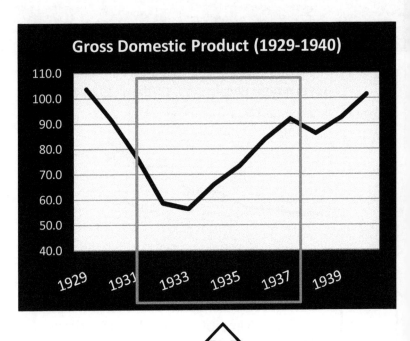

Gross Domestic Product (1929-1940)

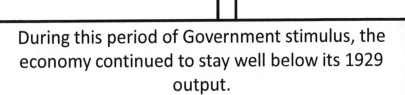

During this period of Government stimulus, the economy continued to stay well below its 1929 output.

If the growth of Gross Domestic Product (GDP) of a country is the first indication of the overall health of an economy, the second measure might be the rate of unemployment.

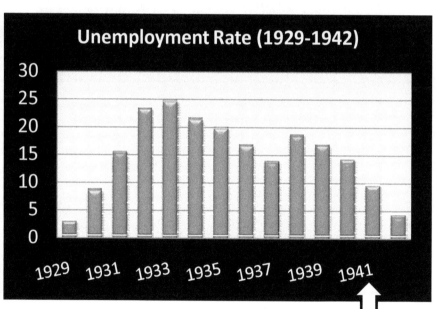

Unemployment Rate (1929-1942)

Yet despite the incredible efforts of the Democratic-led government to create jobs, the unemployment rate didn't drop to "normal" levels until our entrance into World War II.

(1) "Compensation from before World War I through the Great Depression," U.S. Dept. of Labor, Bureau of Labor Statistics, http://www.bls.gov/opub/cwc/cm 20030124ar03p1.htm, accessed 1/31/09

To Review,

15 New Government Agencies
220% increase in Government Spending
68% increase in taxes
$24 billion federal deficit

Q. What ended the great depression?

A. World War II Ended the Great Depression

Most scholars and economists agree that the Great Depression ended because of the huge increase in production directly related to America's entrance into World War II.

In fact, The Library of Congress's "America's Story" website is quoted:

"The end to the Great Depression came about in 1941 with America's entry into World War II."

"The Fed was largely responsible for converting what might have been a garden-variety recession, although perhaps a fairly severe one, into a major catastrophe. Instead of using its powers to offset the depression, it presided over a decline in the quantity of money by one-third from 1929 to 1933 ... Far from the depression being a failure of the free-enterprise system, it was a tragic failure of government."

—Milton Friedman, Two Lucky People, 233

(1) "America's Story, Depression and WWII," America's Library, Library of Congress, http://www.americaslibrary.gov/cgi-bin/page.cgi/jb/wwii, accessed 1/30/09

A brief history of Post WW II Financial Crisis

There have been 18 financial crises post WWII, including the 5 majors (Spain 1977, Norway 1987, Finland 1991, Sweden 1991 and Japan 1992). These crises usually share three characteristics:

1. Housing prices decline 35% over 6 years and stock markets fall 55% over 3.5 years on average.

2. Unemployment rises 7% from the cycle trough over 4 years and GDP output falls an average of 9% averaging 2 years.

and

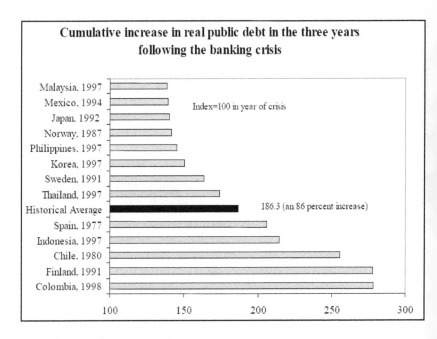

Cumulative increase in real public debt in the three years following the banking crisis

Index=100 in year of crisis

186.3 (an 86 percent increase)

3. Government debt explodes an average 86%.

(1) "The Aftermath of Financial Crisis," as presented to the American Economic Associatio
   1/3/2009,   Carmen Reinhart (U. of Maryland) and Kenneth Rogoff (Harvard U.)

The Japanese Financial Crisis of the 90's and "The Lost Decade"
(which lasted from 1989 – 2005)

CRS Report for Congress

In late 2008, the Congressional Research Service (CRS) submitted a paper detailing the Japanese financial crisis.

History of the Crisis

The report suggests that the cause of the crisis was the Japanese Government's fiscal response to the meteoric rise in both real estate and the stock market: "Japan's monetary authorities flooded the market with liquidity (money) in order to enable businesses to cope with the rising value of the yen."

Results of the Crisis

"By 2000, commercial land values in the six major metropolitan areas had fallen by 80% from their peak level in 1991. Residential and industrial land values also fell by nearly 20%."

"Japan's Nikkei stock market average peaked in 1989 at 40,000 and dropped by 50% in one year. It then plummeted again more than two-thirds to about 12,000 by August 2001."

(1) "The US Financial Crisis: Lessons From Japan," Congressional Research Service, Dick K Nanto, http://fpc.state.gov/documents/organization/110816.pdf, submitted 9/29/08

The Japanese Financial Crisis of the 90's and "The Lost Decade"

Japanese Government Response:

In response to the crisis, Japan:

1. strengthened deposit protection
2. created a provision of emergency liquidity
3. gave assistance to encourage mergers of failed institutions

Later, in 1996, the Government made its first injection of capital by buying bad assets into failing housing lenders, a move that was unpopular among citizens.

1997 brought full systemic financial crisis and the Government injected $2.5B into the system.

Worsening in 1998, Japan nationalized many of their financial institutions and injected another $14B into the system.

By 1999, total stimulus had reached $495B, or 12% of GDP, spent only on banks.

During this period of Crisis, Japan's version of the FDIC issued another $399B, of which $195B was recovered.

(1) "The US Financial Crisis: Lessons From Japan," Congressional Research Service, Dick K. Nanto, http://fpc.state.gov/documents/organization/110816.pdf, submitted 9/29/08

> The steps taken by the Japanese Government (which are believed to have unilaterally perpetuated the crisis, mostly based on their timing) should seem familiar.
>
> Our own government has taken nearly the same steps.

Before the "American Recovery and Reinvestment Act of 2009" was signed into law, the Congressional Budget Office (CBO) drafted a letter to Judd Gregg (Senator, R - NH). Its findings are stated below.

The CBO estimates that the legislation implies an increase in GDP relative to the agency's baseline forecast of between:
- 1.4% and 3.8% by the fourth quarter of 2009.
- 1.1% and 3.3% by the fourth quarter of 2010.
- 0.4% and 1.3% by the fourth quarter of 2011.

Beyond 2014, the legislation is estimated to reduce GDP by between zero and 0.2 percent.

The report goes on to say

The effect on employment is never estimated to be negative, despite lower GDP in later years. **The reduction in GDP is therefore estimated to be reflected in lower wages rather than lower employment,** as workers will be less productive because the capital stock is smaller.

CONGRESSIONAL BUDGET OFFICE

The CBO's goal is to provide "Objective, nonpartisan, and timely analyses to aid in economic and budgetary decisions on the wide array of programs covered by the federal budget and the information and estimates required for the Congressional budget process."

(1) "Estimated Macroeconomic Impacts of H.R. 1 as Passed by the House and by the Senate," Congressional Budget Office, http://www.cbo.gov/ftpdocs/99xx/doc9987/Gregg_Year-by-Year_Stimulus.pdf, accessed 2/16/09

It should be noted that at the onset of the recent financial crises, Washington immediately blamed the greedy private sector. But greed is better associated with government:

The Federal Stimulus bill, signed in February of 2009 by President Obama, contained 7,991 earmarks. (or legislation not tied directly to the intent of the bill, which are usually pet projects given to loyal constituents)

An average of 18 earmarks per member of Congress!

Pres. Obama with impeached Illinois Gov. Rob Blagojevich, who was accused of trying to sell Obama's vacant senate seat.

better man than us proposed that:

individuals should be judged and rewarded based on the content of their character.

The only way to preserve this noble ideal is through the advancement of the free markets and limitation of government.

(1) "Obama to Sign Spending Bill, Push for Earmark Reforms," http://www.foxnews.com/politics/ first100days/2009/03/11/obama-sign-spending-plans-earmark-reforms/100days/, Foxnews.com, Accessed 3/18/09

Chapter
7
Government
Bailouts

What you need to take away

1. Government intervention into the free market historically does not work. The Great Depression is an excellent case study of this point . (page 132-139)

2. The Chrysler bailout of 1979 is often pointed to as a successful Government intervention, but it too did more harm than good. (pages 151-155)

Government Intervention in the free markets has

never worked.

Interventions reward failing companies or industries, penalize those entities viable competitors, and sometimes permanently diminish our country's capacity for growth and competitiveness.

Historically, our government has used times of crisis like the Great Depression and the recession in 2008/09 to push through aggressive interference into the free markets.

One of our <u>most important responsibilities</u> is to stand against government intervention in the free markets!

Cited below are several examples of failed government bailouts.

The First Auto Bailout

After WWII, the biggest challenger to the big 3 was from the <u>Kaiser-Frazer Auto Co.</u> (best known for buying Willy's-Overland, the original maker of Jeep and reinvigorating the brand) founded by entrepreneur Henry Kaiser (of the Kaiser Family Foundation). Getting off to an earlier post-war production than competitors, Kaiser was able to muster production of 100K vehicles and $19 million profit by 1947. (1)

By the late 40's, sales had lagged significantly and the company had become financially weak.

In 1949, the "Reconstruction Finance Corp." (Gov. Agency created in the depression to give loans to private companies) loaned Kaiser $44 M or

$394,000,000 in today's dollars. (2)

Given at below market interest rates, the government loans came with strings attached, including the mandate that a new vehicle (the Henry J) must be sold for $1,300 (or $11,600 in 2008 dollars).

(1) "History of Kaiser Cars 1947-1955," Allpar.com, Kelsey Wright, http://www.allpar.com/cars/adopted/kaiser.html, accessed 2/21/09

(2) Photo, http://www.cartype.com/pics/2989/small/kaiser_buffalo_logo.jpg

(3) "The Reconstruction Finance Corporation's Murky History," Prepared for The Heritage Foundation by Clark Nardinelli Department of Economics Clemson University http://www.heritage.org/Research/Economy/bg317.cfm, accessed 2/21/09

The most important new car in America

Smart
tough
thrifty

To comply with this pricing restriction, Kaiser Auto's Henry J model did <u>not have simple amenities like a glove box, trunk door or sun visors.</u> (1)

After 5 more year of faltering sales, the Kaiser-Frazer Auto Co. ceased passenger car production in 1954, concentrating on the Jeep brand.

In 1970, the stripped down company was bought out by American Motor Co. (A.M.C.) . (2)

Hardly a successful outcome, yet interesting that we don't hear more about this example.

(1) "The 1951 Henry J Models," http://home.comcast.net/~ljfid/hjmodels.htm, accessed 2/21/09
(2) "History of Kaiser Cars 1947-1955." Allpar.com, Kelsey Wright, http://www.allpar.com/cars/adopted/kaiser.html, accessed 2/21/09
(3) Photo Citation,
http://www.oldcarmanualproject.com/brochures/Kaiser/1951/1951 KaiserFrazerand HenryJb/51-02_JPG.html

The Failed Government Bailout of Chrysler

The 1.2 billion dollar bailout (or government-subsidized loan) to the Chrysler Corporation in 1979 is often pointed out as a hugely successful example of how properly timed and implemented federal government intervention in the free markets can be successful.

After faltering sales and dismal profits , the Carter Administration and the Democrat-led Congress pushed through the funding because it was necessary, as Carter said, "to avoid the loss of hundreds of thousands of American jobs among automobile workers <u>and to keep a highly competitive automobile industry in our country."</u> (1) These words are sadly familiar 30 years later.

The bailout is pointed to as a success by elected officials, because with Lee Iacocca steering this listless behemoth, Chrysler was able to pay back the loans sooner than mandated by the government and we are told that "the tax payer profited."

In reality, the bailout was positioned at a time of general economic improvement and had little to do with prudent leadership.

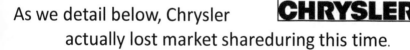

As we detail below, Chrysler actually lost market share during this time.

(1) "Auto Bailout Seems Unlikely," The New York Times, Eduardo Porter, April 14th 2006, http://www.nytimes.com/2006/04/14/automobiles/14bailout.html?pagewanted=print , accessed 2/3/09

(2) " Chrysler LLC," Encyclopedia Britannica, www.britanicca.com , accessed 2/3/09

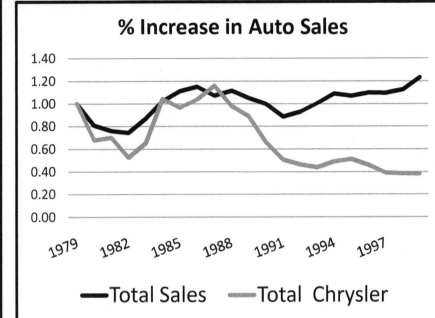

% Increase in Auto Sales

—Total Sales   —Total Chrysler

Despite government intervention, sales at Chrysler slowed faster than the overall market through 1983, or 5 years later, by which time they matched total auto sales, though never surpassing the average industry growth.

In 1999, The Daimler Group (maker of Mercedes) bought the Chrysler Group and merged them into their own operations.
From 1979 – 1999, <u>total auto sales increased 23%.</u>
During the same period,

Chrysler sales decreased 62%.

(1) "US Motor Vehicle Industry, US ,Motor Vehicle Sales 1970-1995," Michigan Senate, http://www.   senate.michigan.gov/sfa/Publications/Issues/MOTORVEH/MOTORVE1.html , accessed 1/30/09
(2) Ward's Automotive Yearbook, Ward's Communications Inc., Detroit Michigan, various years

Case Study — Chrysler Bailout

The result of the 1979 Chrysler Bailout was a less productive and less profitable company.

Worse, though, this blind intervention in the free markets **weakened the American auto industry!**

In the free market economy, companies that are unsuccessful are left to fail and viable companies benefit by taking on the failed company's market share.

While the Government moved to provide aid for Chrysler, they in turn punished the viable GM and Ford.

With an extra $1.2 billion, Chrysler was able to take risks that GM and Ford were not, therefore stealing market share, employees and profit.

Instead of bolstering GM and Ford, these more efficient companies were less competitive.

You might like to know...

Q. Why isn't the American auto industry competitive?
A. Auto Industry's bowing to the federally supported United Autoworkers Union.

UAW members both working and retired pay <u>5%</u> of their health care cost vs. an average <u>30%</u> for the rest of Americans with coverage. (1)

GM, Ford and Chrysler paid UAW members about <u>$75/hour</u> in compensation compared with <u>$45/hour</u> for non UAW auto workers in the US (working in plants owned by foreign manufactures). (2)

The UAW has committed the Big 3 to a Jobs bank that pays laid off employees most of what they earn while they are not working for an indefinite period. (3)

Current Legacy costs (benefits for retirees) cost the Big 3 <u>$3000 per every car sold</u> (3), the avg. cost of a new car sold in the U.S. is $28,400. (4)

or 10.5%

(1) "Restarting Detroit from Washington," Business Week, David Welch and David Riley, 12/22/08 Pg. 34
(2) "For UAW, Aid Likely to Come With Strings," The Wall Street Journal, Kris Maher and Sharon Terlep, 11/21-23/09
(3) " Cutting Worker Costs Key to Automakers' Survival," NPR News, Jenny Gold, http://www.npr.org/templates/story/story.php?storyId=98643230, accessed 2/8/09
(4) "Buying a New Car," Facts for Consumers, Federal Trade Commission, http://www.ftc.gov/bcp/edu/pubs/consumer/autos/aut11.shtm, accessed 2/8/09

On December 19th, 2008 after pressure from a Democratic House, and not wanting to bequeath his successor a bankrupt GM and Chrysler, President Bush repeated the mistake of offering a federal bailout to the auto industry. GM received $9.4 Billion in loans.

Chrysler received $4 Billion in loans.

BUT Ford said it did not need help at this time.

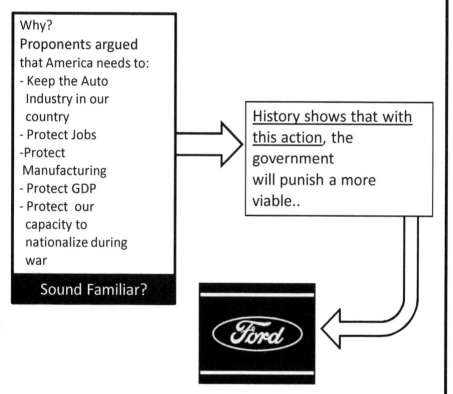

Why?
Proponents argued that America needs to:
- Keep the Auto Industry in our country
- Protect Jobs
- Protect Manufacturing
- Protect GDP
- Protect our capacity to nationalize during war

Sound Familiar?

History shows that with this action, the government will punish a more viable..

(1) "$17.4 billion auto bailout has strings attached," MSNBC, http://www.msnbc.msn.com/id/28311743/, accessed 2/7/09

Conclusion

The government must not interfere with a private economy.

We have noted only a few of the examples showing the failed outcomes of government loans and intervention.

What we have to lose is the foundation of capitalism that has produced the fantastic success that our American economy has enjoyed over the last 150 years, substantially increased wealth for all and the birth of almost all major contributions to science and industry since 1860.

To gain what? A society in parity with the rest of the industrial world, where the wealth and value we've created dissipates to other, freer societies, where capitalism still lives?

Do you think India or China will be more or less "rich" in 10 years? Where will they get this wealth?

The question we must ask is,
        <u>Why are we racing to change the system so drastically that has provided all that we have?</u>

Chapter
8
The Truth About
Climate
Change

What you need to take away

1. The same data that Al Gore uses proves that global climate change isn't man made. (pg. 159-162)

2. Researchers who predicted that average global temperatures would increase at a faster pace have actually shown that the increase is slowing. (pg. 164)

3. A growing number of scientists believe that global climate change isn't man made. (pg. 171-172)

4. The biggest green house gas is water vapor, comprising over 95% of all green house gasses. (pg. 173)

LUNG CANCER CAUSES SMOKING...
HEART ATTACKS CAUSE BLOCKED ARTERIES..
CO_2 CAUSES CLIMATE CHANGE?

Let's take a closer look.

Climate change alarmists tell us man-made CO2 is causing the planet to warm and this will have catastrophic effects.

For this claim to be valid, one must first prove that CO2 causes temperature change.

In his documentary "An Inconvenient Truth," Al Gore uses the Vostok Ice-Core Data to prove this point.

The **Vostok Ice-Core Record** was a collaborative ice-drilling project between Russia, the United States and France at the Russian Vostok station in East Antarctica. It yielded the deepest ice core ever recovered, reaching a depth of 3,623 meters. By careful analysis of this historic ice core, researchers reconstructed trends of temperature and CO2 concentrations over a period of 420,000 years. Data from the Vostok Ice-Core Record can be found at the National Climatic Data Center(http://www.ncdc.noaa.gov/paleo/icecore/antarctica/vostok/vostok.html).

In "An Inconvenient Truth," Al Gore argues that because the two graphs below look like they fit together we must conclude that increases in CO2 cause and increase in temperature.

Data from the Vostok Ice-core

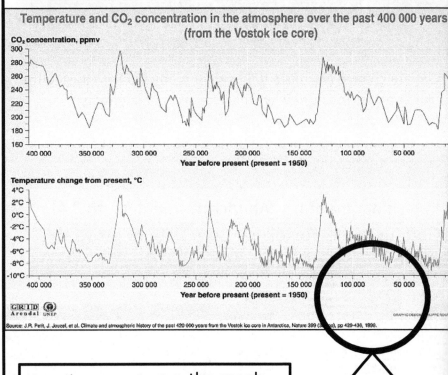

Temperature and CO_2 concentration in the atmosphere over the past 400 000 years (from the Vostok ice core)

Upon closer examination, **the graph uses an axis interval of 50,000 years** (or 9 times longer than written history) which is hugely misleading to the audience because he proposes that the _effect_ of higher temperature follows the _cause_ of increase CO2 by only several years.

AND...

(1) Petit, JR et al. Climate and atmospheric history of the past 420,000 years from the Vostok Ice core, Antartica. *Nature*. 1999:399:429-436.

Scientists know that <u>correlation does not imply causality</u>. To sort out the correlation between CO2 and temperature we must clearly demonstrate what is **CAUSE** and what is **EFFECT**.

Cause comes 1st and effect comes 2nd!

In fact, the authors of the Vostok project conclude that during glacial inception and termination, temperature goes up or down first followed by an increase or decrease in CO2.

At least four other studies confirm the findings of the Vostok ice core record - that atmospheric <u>CO2 content lagged behind shifts in air temperature by 800 to 5,000 years</u>!

1. Fischer H, Wahlen M, Smith J et al. Ice core records of atmospheric CO2 around the last three glacial terminations. *Science*. 2000:283:1712-1714.
2. Indermuhle A, Monnin E, Stauffer B et al. Atmospheric CO2 concentration from 60 to 20 kyr BP from the Taylor Dome ice core, Antartica. *Geophysical Research Letters*. 2000:27:735-738.
3. Monnin E, Inderm A et al. Atmospheric CO2 concentrations over the last glacial termination. *Science*. 2001:291:112-114.
4. Mudelsee M. The phase relations among atmospheric CO2 content, temperature and global ice volume over the past 420 ka. *Quaternary Science Reviews*. 2001:20:583-589.

(1) Petit, JR et al. Climate and atmospheric history of the past 420,000 years from the Vostok ice core, Antartica. *Nature*. 1999:399:429-436.

The correct sequence is:

TEMPERATURE CHANGE CAUSES CO$_2$ CHANGE!

...it also causes climate change

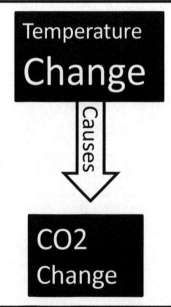

Temperature
Change

Causes

CO2
Change

CO2 DOES NOT DRIVE CLIMATE CHANGE

You might like to know...

Scientists and politicians clinging to global warming alarmism (WHEN PRESSED ON THE ISSUE) claim that even though CO2 is not the primary driver of climate change it is an AMPLIFIER.

However, they hope you never make it this far in the argument, because then they've lost!

To what extent CO2 amplifies temperature is unknown from the historical record. One could just as easily claim CO2 is not an amplifier at all, but a simple bystander of the temperature increase due to increased ocean out gassing of CO2. This is where the argument gets complex.

Climate alarmists are forced to admit that the only proof they have of CO2 being an amplifier of climate change are climate simulations or models.

Regarding models, the following saying applies: **GARBAGE IN, GARBAGE OUT!** If the assumptions that make up a model's algorithms are wrong, then the predictions will obviously be wrong. That being said, a modeler can make a model do anything he/she wants by altering the assumptions.

The only way to judge a model is to compare its predictions against what has actually happened.

So what has actually happened?

You might like to know...

If an environmental alarmist confronts you about temperature change share with them this graph:

A composite index of global mean surface temperature over the last 8 years versus the IPCC global temperature projections

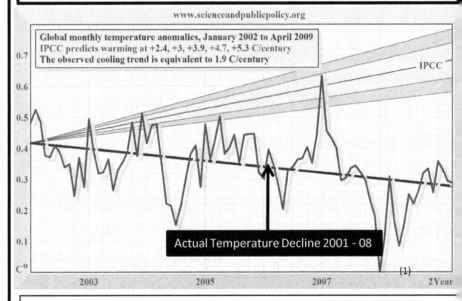

The Science and Public Policy Institute (SPPI) composite index of global mean surface temperature takes the mean of two surface and two satellite data sets (through November 2008) and shows a pronounced downtrend for eight years. No climate models relied upon by the IPCC predicted this downturn.
1. The pink region shows the IPCC's projected rates of temperature increase
2. The real line trend, calculated as the least-squares linear regression on the composite temperature anomalies, *is entirely outside the IPCC's projections*!

(1)Monckton C. Temperature change and CO2 change: a scientific briefing. January 2009.
http://scienceandpublicpolicy.org/images/stories/papers/monckton/temperature_
co2_change_scientific_briefing.pdf.

You might like to know...

Concerned environmentalists used to warn about global warming, but it was soon found that the world is not actually warming. To preserve their hysteria they repackaged their call to arms as "climate change."

The "Climate is Changing" is what we hear everyday,

of course the climate is changing!

But it is almost certainly not a direct result of human action.

IN FACT:

In June of 1974, the *Time* magazine cover story "The Cooling of America" warned of global cooling. In April of 2001 the cover story "A Climate of Despair" warned of global warming.

http://www.time.com/time/magazine/article/0,9171,944914-1,00.html
http://www.time.com/time/magazine/article/0,9171,999631,00.html

"It is the greatest scam in history. I am amazed, appalled, and highly offended by it. Global warming is a scam." (1)

John Coleman, Founder of "The Weather Channel"

(1) As quoted on the "Glenn Beck Show," CNN, 3/5/2008

"The entire North Polar Ice Cap may well be completely gone in 5 years."

- Al Gore

On the far left of environmental activism, Al Gore is the champion of the climate change ideologues. In his widely acclaimed documentary "An Inconvenient Truth," he makes a very pointed and frightening argument that the Earth is on the brink of collapse, caused by man.

But any measurable amount of research clearly shows that the falsified figures and fanatical statements he makes (like the one shown above) are meant as scare tactics.

How can a man who makes such fantastically misleading remarks be taken seriously by any legitimate establishment?

(we encourage you to visit the link below to see for yourself)

(1) The US State Department, Embassy to Norway, http://norway.usembassy.gov /uploads/IV/09/IV 09MZ55175NQCo-asjzSA/Al_Gore_rgb_Ausschnitt_-_i mage_net.jpg, accessed 1/24/09
(2) "Al Gore: The North Polar Ice Cap will Disappear in 5 years," http://www.youtube.com/watch?v=KrPCUWWjh0c, accessed 1/24/09

Temperature change does NOT correlate with hydrocarbon use!
It more likely correlates with solar activity.

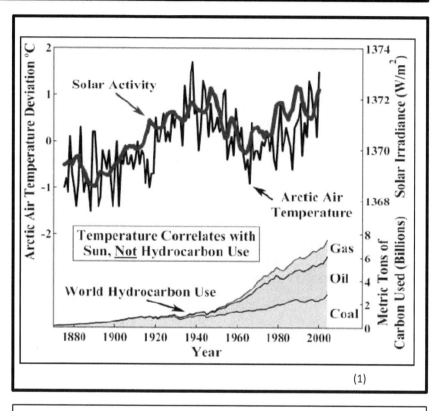

(1)

This figure shows that solar irradiance correlates well with Arctic temperature, while hydrocarbon use does not! This figure draws on three primary sources:

-Soon, W. W.-H. Variable solar irradiance as a plausible agent for multidecadal variations in the Arctic-wide surface air temperature record of the past 130 years, *Geophys. Res. Lett.* (2005):32, L16712, doi:10.1029/2005GL023429.

-Hoyt DV, and Schatten KH. A discussion of plausible irradiance variations. *J. Geophys. Res.* (1993):98:18895-18906.

-Marland G, Boden TA, and Andres RJ. Global, Regional, and National CO2 Emissions. http://cdiac.ornl.gov/trends/emis/tre_glob.htm

(1)Robinson AB, Robinson NE, and Soon W. Environmental Effects of Increased Atmospheric Carbon Dioxide. *Journal of American Physicians and Surgeons.* 2007:12:79-90.

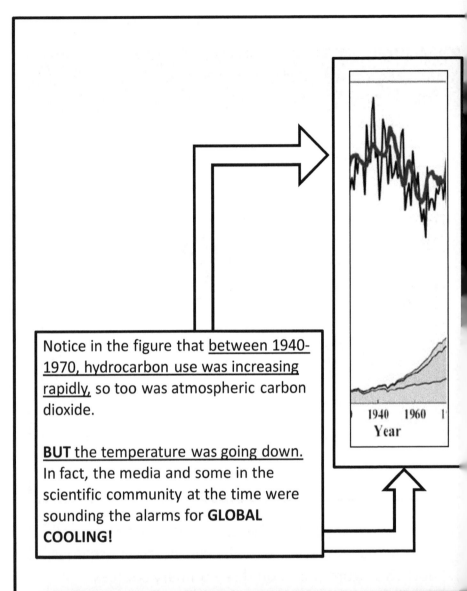

Notice in the figure that <u>between 1940-1970, hydrocarbon use was increasing rapidly,</u> so too was atmospheric carbon dioxide.

BUT <u>the temperature was going down.</u> In fact, the media and some in the scientific community at the time were sounding the alarms for **GLOBAL COOLING!**

IT DOES NOT APPEAR THAT TEMPERATURE IS DIRECTLY RELATED TO CO2, AND IT IS FURTHER PROOF THAT CO2 DOES NOT DRIVE CLIMATE.

(1)Robinson AB, Robinson NE, and Soon W. Environmental Effects of Increased Atmospheric Carbon Dioxide. *Journal of American Physicians and Surgeons*. 2007:12:79-90.

And finally:

While the earth has risen about 0.1 to 0.5 degrees C over the last 100 years, we shouldn't be concerned or surprised.

Viewed through the lens of historical temperature, this is not unusual. The authors of the Vostok ice core record concluded that all four interglacials or warm periods that preceded the Holocene (our current interglacial) were warmer by an average temperature of >2 degrees C. In addition, the authors concluded that our current warm period is the

longest stable warm period recorded in Antarctica during the past 420,000 years (1).

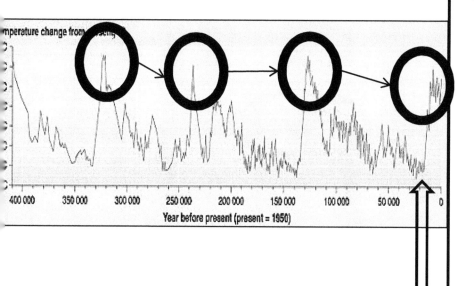

The current warm period is cooler and longer than previous warm periods.

(1) Petit, JR et al. Climate and atmospheric history of the past 420,000 years from the Vostok ice core, Antarctica. *Nature*. 1999:399:429-436.

Past temperature reconstruction from the GRIP ice-core borehole in Greenland.

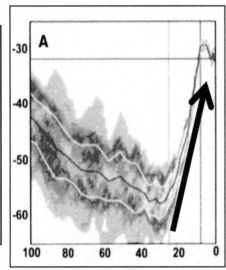

Current warming trends began **20,000** years ago!

This Warm Period is known as the Holocene Maximum

The past 100,000 years until present

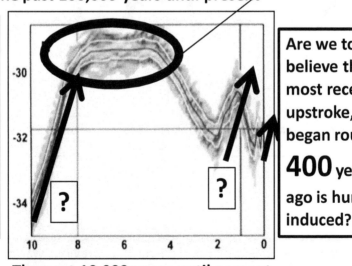

Are we to believe this most recent upstroke, which began roughly 400 years ago is human induced?

The past 10,000 years until present

(1) S. Fred Singer, ed., *Nature, Not Human Activity, Rules the Climate: Summary for Policymakers of the Report of the Nongovernmental International Panel on Climate Change* Chicago, IL: The Heartland Institute, 2008. http://www.sepp.org/publications/NIPCC-Feb%2020.pdf

Poor Argument:
A liberal will say,

"All reputable climate scientists believe in man-made global warming so you should too!"

An excellent reference to refute this claim is the **U. S. Senate Minority Report: More Than 650 International Scientists Dissent Over Man-Made Global Warming Claims,** which can found at the link:

www.epw.senate.gov/minority

This 233 page report, released on December 11th of 2008 presents the compelling truth, that many very prominent, international climate scientists *DON'T AGREE WITH THE HYPE REGARDING MAN-MADE GLOBAL WARMING!*

It's best to read it yourself and draw your own conclusions.

Professor William Happer's statement to the U.S. Senate on February 25, 2009 Happer is the Cyrus Fogg Bracket Professor of Physics at Princeton University. He was also the Director of Energy Research at DOE from 1990-93, where he supervised all of DOE's work on climate change. He states:

"The climate is warming and CO2 is increasing. Doesn't this prove that CO2 is causing global warming through the greenhouse effect? No, *the current warming period began about 1800 at the end of the little ice age, long before there was an appreciable increase of CO2.* There have been similar and even larger warmings several times in the 10,000 years since the end of the last ice age. These earlier warmings clearly had nothing to do with the combustion of fossil fuels. The current warming also seems to be due mostly to natural causes, not to increasing levels of carbon dioxide. *Over the past ten years there has been no global warming, and in fact a slight cooling. This is not at all what was predicted by the IPCC models.*"

On sea level rise:

"The sea level is indeed rising, just as it has for the past 20,000 years since the end of the last ice age. *Fairly accurate measurements of sea level have been available since about 1800. These measurements show no sign of any acceleration.*"

(1) Happer W. Climate Change. Statement Before the U.S. Senate Environment and Public Works Committee Senator Barbara Boxer, Chair . 2/25/09. http://www.marshall.org/pdf/materials/629.pdf. Accessed 3/2/09

You might like to know...

Water Vapor rules the greenhouse system, accounting for **95%** of ALL Atmospheric Greenhouse Gases.

Water vapor is **99.999%** of Natural Origin! (1)

CO_2 accounts for 3.6% of all atmospheric greenhouse gases. Out of this 3.6%, <u>man contributes ONLY 3.2% of this!</u>

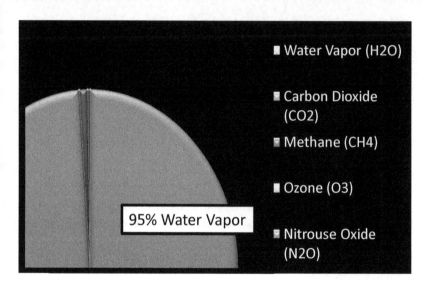

- Water Vapor (H_2O)
- Carbon Dioxide (CO_2)
- Methane (CH_4)
- Ozone (O_3)
- Nitrouse Oxide (N_2O)

95% Water Vapor

In conclusion, humans contribute much less than 1% (0.28%) to the total greenhouse gas effect. Reducing human CO_2 emissions would have a large impact on standard of living but a NEGLIGIBLE impact on climate change.

1. http://www.geocraft.com/WVFossils/greenhouse_data.html. Accessed 2/10/09

It is important to note that everyone, both liberal and especially conservative, wants to pass on a healthy environment to the next generation but we forget that...

The ideal of environmental preservation was pioneered by conservatives.

Theodore Roosevelt (a republican

is often revered as "The father of conservation." An avid hunter and outdoorsman, he said:

"I recognize the right and duty of this generation to develop and use the nature resources of our land: but I do not recognize the right to waste them, or to rob, by wasteful use, the generations that come after us."

Roosevelt also:
- Formed the Forestry Service (later the NPA)
- Increased forest reserves by 500%
- Created the first National Park (five in total) and a total of 18 national monuments. (1)

(1) "Theodore Roosevelt," The National Park Service, **http://www.nps.gov/history/l logcabin/html/tr.html** accessed 1/24/09

Chapter
9
Responsible
Energy Policies

1. President Obama's proposal of a cap and trade policy that will reward companies for curbing carbon output will be a middle class tax increase. (page 178)

2. We have the ability to create energy independence and to even become an exporter of energy. (pages 182-188)

NO energy legislation should be passed in which the goal of the legislation is to decrease CO2 emissions!

Conservatives must fight legislation that would increase taxation on companies or individuals for emitting over a certain amount of CO2, as well as legislation which would require companies or individuals to buy the rights to emit CO2.

This legislation is better known as
"Cap and Trade."

CO2 does NOT cause climate change, therefore policies to decrease CO2 emissions are harmful to the economic recovery and future growth of our country!

The 2 Problems with Cap and Trade

1. The Congressional Budget Office (CBO) estimated that the value of the allowances under the cap and trade proposal that went to the Senate floor in June 2008, would be roughly *$112 billion* once the cap took effect in 2012 and would increase as the cap became more stringent. (1)

Think of it as a $112 billion dollar tax (or 10%) increase!

This tax increase will affect every single person in America because in some way or another, everyone uses fossil fuels or reaps their benefits either directly or indirectly.

2.

If the United States joins Europe in the failed "Cap and Trade" tax, it will still leave 60% of carbon producers without such regulation and at a competitive advantage!

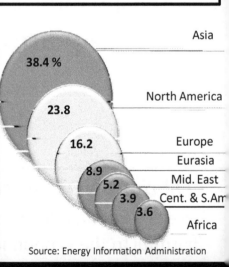

Asia — 38.4 %

North America — 23.8

Europe — 16.2

Eurasia — 8.9

Mid. East — 5.2

Cent. & S.Am — 3.9

Africa — 3.6

Source: Energy Information Administration

China and India and others have no such tax!

(1) Orszag PR. Issues in designing a cap-and-trade program for carbon dioxide emissions. 9/18/08. http://www.cbo.gov/ftpdocs/97xx/doc9727/09-18_ClimateChange_Testimony.pdf. Accessed 3/5/09

Alternative Energy

Pursuing alternative energy choices is a reasonable policy objective of the Obama administration, but not because it reduces carbon emissions.

Becoming producers of alternative energy technologies could lead to:

1. Substantial economic growth over time for our country.
2. Reduced reliance on foreign energy.

It is worth noting that President George W. Bush shared President Obama's opinion on alternative energy production.

During his address to Congress in February of 2009, President Barack Obama declared, "We will double this nation's supply of renewable energy in the next three years."

"From 2005 to 2007, [George Bush] oversaw a **near-doubling** of the electrical output from solar and wind power. And **between 2007 and 2008, output from those sources grew by another 30%.**" [1]

(1) Bryce R. Let's get real about renewable energy.
http://online.wsj.com/article/SB123621221496034823.html. Accessed 3/5/09

You might like to know...

Since 1978, the Federal Gov. has legislated no less than 15 pro-ethanol laws.

Let us not forget the lessons we've learned about government intervention in the free markets!

Guaranteed Loans to producers

Subsidies to buyers

Tariffs for importers

$3 Billion a year

- If every farmable acre was used for ethanol production, it would replace only 12.3% of gasoline consumption.
- Corn based ethanol yields only 25% more energy than it costs to produce (oil yields 8.3 +/- times the energy to produce)
- Ethanol only generates 12% less green house gases than gasoline and produces more smog pollutants!

All for a fuel that consumes 80% of the energy it takes to make it the fuel!

(1) "Study: Ethanol Won't Solve Energy Problems," The Washington Post, H. Joseph Herbert, The AssociatedPress, http://www.washingtonpost.com/wp-dyn/content/article/2006/07/10/AR2006071000788.html, Accessed, 3/23/09
(2) http://tonto.eia.doe.gov/energy_in_brief/energy_subsidies.cfm
(3) http://www.eia.doe.gov/kids/history/timelines/ethanol.html

The Truth:

We can make HUGE gains in alternative energy but we will still depend on hydrocarbons!

The latest data from the U.S. Energy Information Administration shows that total solar and wind output for 2008 was likely to be about **45,493,000** megawatt-hours.

Out of: **4,118,198,000** total megawatt-hours

for a grand total of **1.1%**

Solar and wind sources are providing the equivalent of *76,000 barrels of oil per day*.

America consumes about **47.4 million barrels of oil equivalent per day.** (1)

(1) Bryce R. Let's get real about renewable energy. 3/5/09.
(2) http://online.wsj.com/article/SB123621221496034823.html. Accessed 3/5/09

Q. What can we do NOW in the interest of Energy Independence?

A. Make use of **ALL** our natural resources from *sea to shining sea!*

OIL

COAL

NATURAL GAS

Two-thirds of the energy Americans use is either from oil or natural gas. High oil and natural gas prices are mostly the result of a supply and demand imbalance. As world-wide demand for energy has increased we haven't increased our domestic supply of oil and natural gas.

Meanwhile, the production of our domestic oil and natural gas resources is declining. <u>We can reverse this trend.</u>

> 1st: The U.S. has the highest coal reserves in the world.
> 3rd: The U.S. third highest natural gas reserves.
> 17th: The U.S. seventeenth highest oil reserves. (1) (2)

(1) Encyclopaedia Britannica, "Coal" and "Natural Gas," accessed 3/22/09, www.britannica.com
(2) Wikipedia.com, "Oil Reserves," Accessed 3/22/09, http://en.wikipedia.org/wiki/Oil_reserves

The U.S. Minerals Management Service and U.S. Geological Survey estimate (mean value) that approximately **29 billion barrels (BBls) of oil** and **94 trillion cubic feet (TcF) of gas** have been off limits to industry due to leasing moratoria. However, estimation of these resources has significantly increased with almost every survey done. Therefore, using historical trend data, it can be extrapolated that there is an even larger amount of undiscovered resources...*as high as 94 BBls of oil and 212 TcF of gas!* (1)

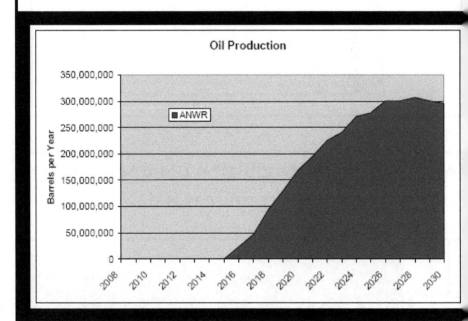

(1) Vidas H, Hugman B. Strengthening Our Economy: The Untapped U.S. Oil and Gas Resources. http://energytomorrow.org/ViewResource.ashx?id=5270. accessed 3/5/0⁴

Natural gas is a clean-burning fuel choice that powers most new homes and buildings, as well as power plants, but government policies have been inconsistent. Policymakers and environmentalists have traditionally encouraged natural gas use because it was clean-burning and abundant in the U.S. However, *the same groups have discouraged the exploration and production of new domestic gas supplies.* This paradox creates another supply-demand imbalance. The increase in natural gas demand isn't being met with new supplies. *It doesn't have to be this way.*

This is just from the Outer Continental Shelf

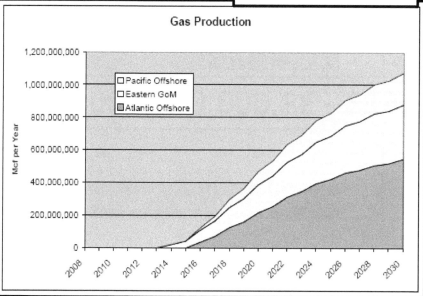

(1) Vidas H, Hugman B. Strengthening Our Economy: The Untapped U.S. Oil and Gas Resources. http://energytomorrow.org/ViewResource.ashx?id=5270. accessed 3/5/09

Here are some of the projected economic impacts of private sector spending in **2020** if drilling bans were lifted on ANWR, OCS (Pacific and Atlantic offshore and the Eastern Golf of Mexico) and the Rocky Mountains. (1)

Total Number of New Jobs Created:

110,000 – 160,000

Total Economic Output :

$23 - 33,000,000,000,000

(that's Trillion)

Total Number of Polar Bears Killed:

0

(that's zero)

ANWR – Arctic National Wildlife Reserve
OCS – Outer Continental Shelf

(1) Vidas H, Hugman B. Strengthening Our Economy: The Untapped U.S. Oil and Gas Resources. http://energytomorrow.org/ViewResource.ashx?id=5270. accessed 3/5/0

Clean Coal – how about we use more of this?

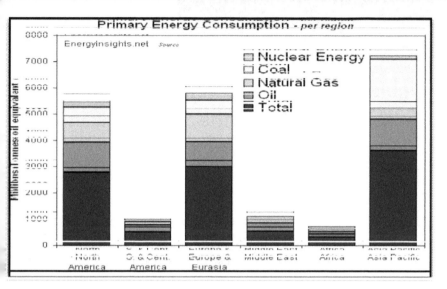

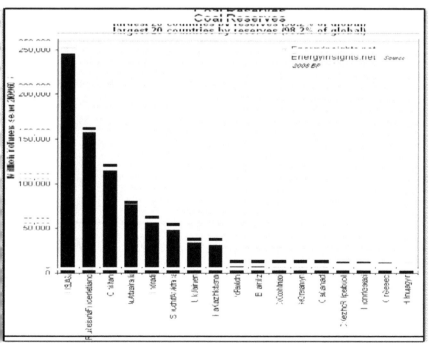

(1) http://www.energyinsights.net/cgi-script/csArticles/articles/000001/000118.htm.
Accessed 3/9/09

Coal = Motor Fuel
Who Knew?

Liquid fuel was made from coal as long ago as World War II, and the South African company "SASOL" does it now.

Elliot Kennel, the administrative coordinator for carbon products research at West Virginia U., is a nuclear engineer and physicist with a background in carbon nanomaterials. He sees liquid fuels from coal as a next step on the way to a hydrogen economy.

"I think ultimately we will be using more and more hydrogen and less fossil fuels, **but I don't foresee the need for fossil fuels going away soon ...**I think we're going to continue to grow our economy with liquid fuels for 10 or 20 years."

... A REASONABLE MAN

(1) http://www.redorbit.com/news/science/222728/wvu_researcher_sees_coals_
    potential_as_motor_fuel/. Accessed 3/9/09

Here's the Point

We understand, and hope you do too, that fossil fuels can't last forever and their supplies will eventually be exhausted. We also recognize that hydrogen, wind and solar power represent the future for energy production across the world. However, alternative energy sources aren't viable yet from a cost perspective. Eventually they will be, and when that occurs we hope that a variety of energy products exist to maximize quality and competitiveness within the energy market. This is best for consumers and it is ultimately best for the competitiveness of our country.

The question remains, how do we get from here to there? By taxing viable energy sources that emit an invisible gas out of existence? By providing a bear market for some propped up, government-funded alternative energy company to come along and fill that gap?

What about questions regarding our immediate economic conditions? Do we prevent a legitimate industry from creating wealth and jobs for the citizens of this country? Do we appease radical leftists, most of whom can't present one compelling point in favor of man-made global warming? Do we make more and more citizens reliant on big government because they can't afford skyrocketing energy bills due to new cap and trade policies?

Don't be afraid to challenge your peers on this topic. Our logic is sound, and if you present compelling arguments against man-made global warming and in favor of domestic energy production, you will not lose.

Chapter 10 Conclusion

"Remember,

Democracy never lasts long.

It soon wastes, exhausts and murders itself. There has never been a Democracy yet that did not commit Suicide."

- John Adams
April, 1814 in a letter to Thomas Jefferson

"A democracy cannot last. Its nature ordains, that its next charge shall be into a military despotism, of all known governments, perhaps, the most prone to shift its head, and the slowest to mend its vices. The reason is that the tyranny of what is called the people, and that by the sword, both operate alike to debase and corrupt, till there are neither men left with the spirit to desire liberty, nor morals with the power to sustain justice."

- Fisher Ames (U.S. Congress 1789-97)
The Dangers of American Liberty, 1805

As we discussed in the first chapter, our Founders created a Republic (not a Democracy) to protect inalienable rights through a constitution to prevent this inevitable outcome. Unfortunately, we too often neglect the values our Republic was founded upon, choosing to believe that we live in a democracy .

. Image citation: National Park Service, http://www.nps.gov/adam/planyourvisit/things
. "The Quotable Founding Fathers", Fall River Press 2008
. http://bioguide.congress.gov/scripts/biodisplay.pl?index=A000174, Accessed 10/2/09

The founders great concern was that despite their warnings and best laid plans this nation would succumb to the same pitfalls that toppled every previous democracy.

This concept is well summarized by Alexander Tytler

The following quotation is surrounded by speculation regarding its origin, but is most often attributed to Alexander Tytler.

Tytler was a Scottish-born (1747) lawyer and writer and this quotation is thought to first have been attributed to him on March 5, 1964, by Ronald Reagan at a speech given at a Barry Goldwater rally. (1)

(1) "The Truth about Tytler," Loren Collins, http://www.lorencollins.net/tytler.html, accessed 1/17/09

A democracy is always temporary in nature: it simply cannot exist as a permanent form of government. A democracy will continue to exist up until the time that voters discover that they can vote themselves generous gifts from the public treasury. From that moment on, the majority always votes for the candidates who promise the most benefits from the public treasury, with the result that every democracy will finally collapse due to loose fiscal policy, which is always followed by a dictatorship. The average age of the world's greatest civilizations from the beginning of history has been about 200 years. During those 200 years, these nations always progressed through the following sequence:

- Alexander Fraser Tytler

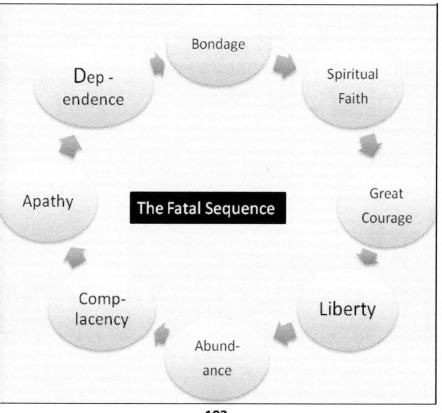

If it is true that democracies have a finite life span, at what stage is the United States?
Will we and our children have more opportunity and success than our parents and grandparents did? If not, what has changed?

In a recent Rasmussen poll, only *20%* of American adults believe that today's children will be better off than their parents, while *62%* believed they would NOT!

"62% Say Today's Children Will Not Be Better off Than Their Parents," Rasmussen Reports, 10/4/2009

The most important variable that has changed is the increased role that government plays in our lives, and more specifically the fully unsuitable rate at which it spends our money at the expense of personal liberty.

Increase in Government Spending

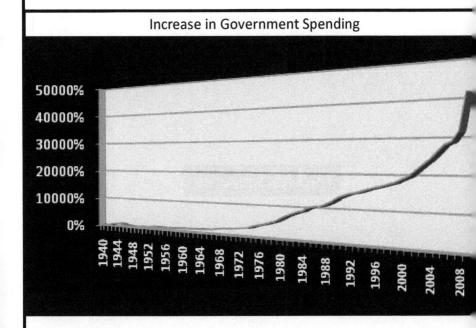

This spending is shouldered by the taxpayers, and more specifically the burden falls to our generation.

National Debt per Citizen

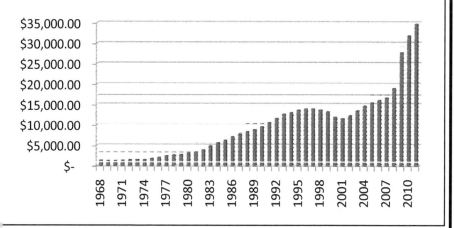

The total debt that the Federal Government has taken out in our names now amounts to $12.1 T (3) (or $87K per worker) and

the interest owed each year on the debt by every working man and woman alone amounts to $1,820 (4).

In perspective, the 2008 median household income in the United States was $61,521 (5). This $1,820 owed solely to service the debt is 2.96% of that average family's pay.

While seemingly small compared to the multitude of sales, income, state, local, property and other taxes we pay today, the Federal Government's historic level of taxation (as a percentage of GDP) did not permanently move above the 3% level until our entrance into World War I, or for the first 143 years of our history.

1) "Debt Held by the Public 68 - 07," Congressional Budget Office, http://www.cbo.gov/budget/data/historical.pdf, accessed 12/14/09
2) "National and State Population Estimates," National Census Bureau, http://www.census.gov/popest/states/NST-ann-est.html, accessed 12/14/09
3) "US National Debt Clock," http://www.brillig.com/debt_clock/, accessed 12/14/09
4) "A New Era of Responsibility," 2009 Federal Budget, http://www.whitehouse.gov/omb/assets/fy2010_new_era_a_new_era_of_responsibilit y2.pdf, accessed 12/14/09
5) "Median and Mean Income," Census Bureau, http://www.census.gov/hhes/www /income/histinc/f07AR.xls, accessed 12/14/09.

Through the increases in spending, the United States government has become the largest "business" or economic entity in the world. Total government spending in 2009 is expected to be $6,143 billion or an estimated 230% more than China spends; the world's next largest economy (with 300% more people).

Who is at the helm of this financial juggernaut? The majority of our Senators are Attorneys (58) or career government employees (13) who have little or no direct business experience. Is it any wonder that our elected officials display a lack of understanding of the most basic laws of economics and business?

Over the last several decades, our representatives have expanded the welfare state while promising us we would never feel the pain of these government handouts. It might be fair to say that these easy spenders bought the votes of yesterday's elections at the expense of tomorrow's generations. Under the surface, the debt that they have regimentally added to year after year is sinking our ship.

It is important to know that the government can't actually "print" money without the dire consequence of inflation (which is deadly to politicians). Instead, new debt is created and purchased with existing money that can be spent by the government.

What happens if we can't find buyers for this new debt? After all, we have increased our debt significantly over the last two years. China and the rest of the world's appetite for our debt is finite.

In December of 2009 the world debt markets were rocked because Greece's credit rating was cut. The turmoil was caused because lower ratings mean higher probability of default on Greece's debt, threatening inflation, government bankruptcy and worse. Of note, the downgrade resulted because Greece has a government budget deficit of 13% of GDP (according to Business Week, 12/21/09) and total debt that amounts to 113% of total economic production for one year. The United State's budget deficit for fiscal year 2009 (which ended in Sept) is 10% of GDP and total debt will amount to 100% of GDP if the ceiling is increased. The dangers of increased spending are perhaps closer than we care to admit.

(1) US Senate Website , http://www.senate.gov/general/contact_
     information/senators_cfm.cfm, accessed 12/1/09

As the chart below shows, our representatives can raise the total amount of debt that we hold anytime that they choose. On December 10th of 2009, they raised the "debt ceiling" for the 9th time this decade to $14T; a total 140% increase.

If we cannot find purchasers of our debt, the economic, political and fundamental risks will shake the foundation of our country with a ferocity worse that the great depression; a shift from which our nation might not recover.

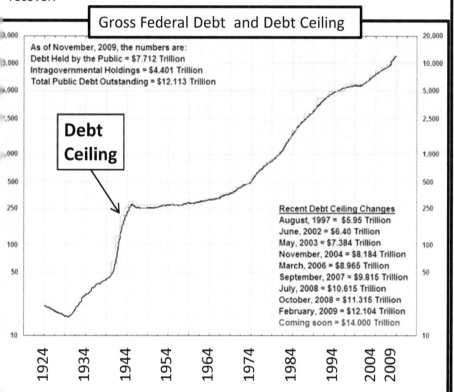

Gross Federal Debt and Debt Ceiling

As of November, 2009, the numbers are:
Debt Held by the Public = $7.712 Trillion
Intragovernmental Holdings = $4.401 Trillion
Total Public Debt Outstanding = $12.113 Trillion

Debt Ceiling

Recent Debt Ceiling Changes
August, 1997 = $5.95 Trillion
June, 2002 = $6.40 Trillion
May, 2003 = $7.384 Trillion
November, 2004 = $8.184 Trillion
March, 2006 = $8.965 Trillion
September, 2007 = $9.815 Trillion
July, 2008 = $10.615 Trillion
October, 2008 = $11.315 Trillion
February, 2009 = $12.104 Trillion
Coming soon = $14.000 Trillion

"I wish it were possible to obtain a single amendment to our constitution. I would be willing to depend on that alone for the reduction of the administration of our government to the genuine principles of its constitution; I mean an additional article, taking from the federal government the power of borrowing."

- Thomas Jefferson, 1798

(1) "Gross Federal Debt and Debt Ceiling," Ron Griess, www.thechartstore.com, accessed 12/15/09
(2) "The Quotable Founding Fathers", Fall River Press 2008

"**Freedom is never more than one generation away from extinction.** We didn't pass it on to our children in the bloodstream. It must be fought for, protected, and handed on for them to do the same, or one day we will spend our sunset years telling our children and our children's children what it was once like in the United States where men were free."

While history is a metric to use and learn from, it cannot be used to predict the future. It is not too late to significantly slow the rate of decay or even to stop it all together!

The surest means by which to prevent this historical outcome is to learn the threats to our Republic and teach our peers through the means of thoughtful and educated debate.

Notes on Debating

Debating

You now have the most effective tool in the world: knowledge. But, with knowledge comes the charge to do something worthwhile with it. Knowing how to present your ideas is as important (yes, we said as important) as knowing the facts. If you don't believe us, simply think back to President Obama's campaign; it was full of promise and never really delivered a plan of action, but his message was delivered more perfectly (though not as well as Clinton or Reagan) than McCain's and he won. He was never confrontational, never let himself get upset and never got off message. This is how you convince people, and we can learn from his playbook.

As a result of Obama's campaign, our liberal contemporaries are driven by one word slogans (hope and change) and, to a greater degree, emotion. Their arguments and beliefs are rooted in these emotions:
- We need government health care because we need to help everyone
- We need to stop the evil coal companies to stop global warming
- We need change (This was he most common reason given when voters were asked why they voted for Barack Obama, but when pressed, often couldn't identify what change they meant)

We can not fight emotional arguments with emotional arguments!

Because their beliefs are rooted in emotion, we cannot battle them with emotion. We must take the higher ground intellectually, and debate them using a tested strategy. Fighting emotion with emotion will never further our ideals.

The goal is not just to win an argument. In the classic "How to Win Friends and Influence People" (awful title but tremendous book), which has sold at least 15 million copies, the author, Dale Carnegie, says :

"You can't win an argument. You can't because if you lose it, you lose it; and if you win it, you lose it."

What he means is that if you use your new found knowledge to soundly defeat every liberal you meet by showing them how wrong they are, they will resent you, and we will gain nothing. Our goal must be instead to have a conversation, not to win an argument. When managed correctly, a better outcome will be observed.

Debating

The best way to leverage understanding is to draw similarities between ourselves and those of liberal philosophy; first to ourselves and then outwardly to our peers. After all, liberals and conservatives want the same outcome: the betterment of our country. The difference is how we chart the path to get there and how we define betterment.

Outlined here is a strategy that will work to further our cause and persuade our peers. If these steps are followed closely, you will meet with success.

1. **Understanding:** The most difficult human quality that we should all hope to master is that of understanding. To understand why a liberal feels the way they do will help us to best unwind their arguments.
I understand how you feel (or think) about – issue - , I really do.
I used to feel (or think) the same way.
What I found (or learned) was that – insert fact here.

   Remember, you can't convince all of the people all of the time, <u>BUT</u> you will be surprised at how powerful the above strategy is when paired with the facts and figures you now know.

2. **Never be defensive; never raise your voice:** Only after we exercise understanding can we lay the foundation of assimilation. When we first begin a conversation with a liberal it is easy to have our ire drawn up by their lack of logical reason; it happens to us all the time. Our first thought is to raise our voice, talk over them, and have our points heard. If we get defensive, or tell them immediately that they are wrong, we fight emotion with emotion and cannot hope to win. Let the person who is wrong talk out their ideas.

   The goal is not to have the other person raise their voice either. If they do, their defenses have already been alarmed and they are no longer listening to your points. If, however, your goal is to let off some steam then have at it.

3. **Let them do 60% of the talking:** The Greek philosopher Epictetus said "we have two ears and only one mouth so we listen twice and speak once." Only after you have listened earnestly to what the other person has said can you best prepare your remarks. Only after you have listened earnestly will their defenses come down.

Debating

4. **Lead them with yeses:** In one of the best books written on selling, "How to Master the Art of Selling" (New York: Warner, 2005), Tom Hopkins said, "When I say it, they tend to doubt it. When they say it, it's true." What he means is that when you "tell" someone something, they hear you saying that they're wrong. Instead, if you can lead them to your conclusion with simple closing questions that demand a yes answer you can build towards agreements. For example, you can say:
   · Don't you agree that it's important to protect the environment?
   · Wouldn't you agree that our climate is changing?
   · Isn't it true that man has only been producing large amounts of carbon for 100 years?
   · You know that there have been significant cooling trends over the last 400,000 years don't you?

   Now prove it to them, but don't tell them you're going to prove it to them: You have measured your tone and followed a proven strategy, now show them the facts. You'll only have time for one or two before they stop listening, so make them good.

   Before you do share the facts, remember not to say "let me prove/show/tell you...," no one wants to be told anything. That is the same thing as telling them they are wrong; their defenses have gone up; you've wasted 20 minutes.

   Instead say, "let me share with you," or better yet use the classic selling technique of the feel/felt/found:

   "I understand how you <u>feel</u>, I once <u>felt</u> the same way, what I <u>found</u> was that..."

   ### Example:

   Recently I was walking down the street of an affluent Philadelphia suburb past a Starbucks when a young man armed with a smile and a clip board stopped me. On summer break and with nothing better to do he asked me if I was interested in joining a group dedicated to stopping global warming. Instead of being put off by him, I viewed it as an opportunity for assimilation!

Debating

Here's how the conversation went;

He: Excuse me, do you have a minute for the environment?

I: Of course.

He: I'm part of a national organization dedicated to stopping global warming caused by greenhouse gasses. We're collecting email addresses so we can let you know when there is a meeting or other activity (as he handed me the clipboard).

I: (taking the clipboard) Sounds great, but I didn't know that man made CO_2 caused global warming …

He: (in an excited voice he gave me his prepared answer) It definitely does! According to scientific data collected from all over the world, surface temperatures are increasing rapidly. If it continues, many species will die, ice caps will melt and oceans will rise! (by listening 60% of the time I was able to formulate my angle)

I: From the CO_2 caused by man (starting to lead him with yeses)?

He: Yes

I: That's what Al Gore's movie was about right?

He: Yes

I: Did you see it?

He: Of course, it's the reason why I decided to become active!

I: That's great. Yeah, the climate is changing isn't it?

He: Definitely.

I: (now there are about ten major points that you can try to make, but I'd get one or maybe two in) In Al Gore's movie he showed the correlation between CO_2 in the atmosphere and temperature change over what, 400,000 years right?

He: Yes

I: But man has only been producing large amounts carbon for about 100 years right?

He: Well, yes.

I: I suppose you would have to agree that because man made CO_2 accounts for only 1/1000th of the CO_2 in the atmosphere and that the Earth has had a changing climate for 400,000 years, that the climate change we have today most likely isn't man made? (or insert your own point)

He: Actually I don't agree.

I: Well, to be honest I didn't expect you to. But I do understand how you feel, I once felt the same way. I found after doing some research that I was wrong. I hope you do too before you waste more time being misinformed (handing back the clipboard).